Island Explorer

Surfing, sailing and exploring
beyond Sumatra and the Mentawai Islands

by Dan Scheffler

Editors: Claire Strombeck and David Tyfield

Cover Design: Justin Groombridge

Photos: Dan Scheffler, unless otherwise credited

Published by Trippy Books

Copyright Dan Scheffler 2012

Table of Contents

To view photographs of the journey, go to
www.facebook.com/pages/
Dan-Scheffler/521593047867330

Vir Pappa.
Jy het my geleer van die see en my lus gemaak om te reis.

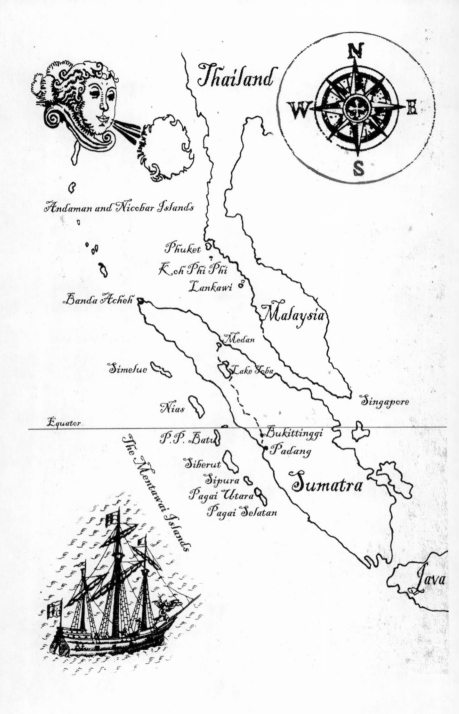

The names of the characters and the ship have been changed to protect the author (who is innocent).

"I travel not to go anywhere, but to go. I travel for travel's sake. The great affair is to move."

Robert Louis Stevenson

Prologue
The Trans-Sumatran Highway

"I had endured the Trans-Sumatran Highway and I swore that I would never ever in my life attempt anything like it again."

The bus driver slammed on brakes and we came to a screeching halt by the side of the road, setting off a cacophony of squawking chickens, bleating goats and swearing passengers. I craned my neck to see what had happened, but the only reason for stopping was that our driver had spotted more people who wanted to travel to somewhere along our route. He was happy to pocket a few more Rupiah in fares and to let them squeeze inside. After all, he had his own seat all to himself. A barrage of hooting and shouting came from the vehicles in the traffic behind us as the bus swerved onto the road again.

We were on the Trans-Sumatran Highway heading for the mountains and this part of my journey had not gotten off to a good start.

I had landed at the town of Parapat, on the shore of the picturesque Lake Toba, after taking a ferry from the island in the middle of the huge water-filled volcanic crater. My next stop was Bukittinggi, but the lady at the bus station shook her head sadly when she saw my surfboards. The busses that went south did not take that kind of luggage and she did not know of an alternative way to get there. She shrugged her shoulders and then just ignored me. The woman in the line behind me at the ticket counter shuffled past and pushed me aside, ending my enquiry.

I sat around for a while, wondering what to do, when I heard the greeting that every traveller to Indonesia gets to know so well: "Hello Mister". "Hello Mister" is used to address any foreign man or woman. This usually signals an intention to practice English with you, or it's just a simple greeting. However, it can also mean, "I am a crook and I am now going to get as much money from you as possible, you stupid tourist." The man who approached me fell into the latter category of Hello-Misterers. I could see it in his eyes and he knew that I knew that he was about to work me over. But he also knew that it was almost getting dark and that I did not want to spend an evening on the street in Parapat, or probably worse, in one of the cheaper local "hotels". So with this unspoken understanding between us, knowing that he had me by the crown jewels, he proceeded to twist and squeeze. There were no regular busses that would take my surfboards to Bukittinggi, he said, but he knew of one that, by a very fortunate coincidence, was leaving for just that town tonight. He could arrange for my boards to be transported. This kind of allowance was not usually made, but he knew the driver and he could persuade him to take me along, at the right price of course. I had to understand that they would be making a special concession for me, so there would be a nominal extra charge.

What choice did I have? I had already spoken to some of the regular bus drivers directly and they were not prepared to take my surfboards, even after I had offered extra payment. Nobody could tell me of any alternative transport. My new agent smiled broadly, showing off a mishmash of gold teeth, ill-fitting dentures and tobacco stained gums. I smiled back at him, while trying to convert Rupiah to a more familiar currency in my mind, comparing his price to the cost of a regular ticket and thinking murderous thoughts. We finally agreed on a price and, after I had paid up, we walked around the corner to a questionable looking coach that was about to leave "any minute now". I loaded my board bag onto the roof and found my way onto the bus. There were no luggage racks inside the bus and most people kept their bags on their laps. I put my twenty-kilogram backpack on the floor next to me and waited for the bus to leave.

Three hours later, after slowly filling up with people, livestock and luggage, it wheezed and coughed out of the bus station and lurched into the path of an oncoming truck, setting the tone for the rest of the journey.

I soon found out that I was on a local bus, which was really only meant for short distance travel; but it did go all the way to my destination. The local bus will never refuse one more passenger and it is always overcrowded. Everybody on the local bus chain-smokes clove cigarettes. The people here hate open windows and as soon as I opened one for some fresh air, it would be closed again. The offended person would indicate to me that the cold wind would aggravate his chest problems. The notion that cigarettes could be harmful to your health seems unheard of in Sumatra.

The first four hours of the trip were okay. Of course, everyone wanted to talk to the white tourist and they rotated through the seat next to me continuously. Within half an hour I got my first marriage proposal. As I would find out over the next weeks, this particular lady was by no means the only person who would suggest matrimony to complete strangers like me, but she was the most persistent. It went like this:

"Hello mister!"

"Hello."

"How are you?"

"Fine and you?"

"I am more wonderful! Are you married?"

"No."

"You have girlfriend?"

"Yes."

"But she no here?"

"No."

"Good! Will you marry me?"

"Well, um, I don't know you at all. What would your father say?"

"He like very much." She turned to indicate an elderly gentleman sitting next to his wife a few rows behind us. He flashed me an encouraging betel nut-smile. She continued, "I get to know you well on this bus. We have many hours together!"

My heart sank. "But I'm not Muslim."

"No problem. We have very good Imam. He cut you quickly, snip-snip, and he teach you Koran. My brothers also help you." She pointed out three sinister looking fellows, who did not return my nervous smile. "Look, I have strong back, wide hips, thick legs!" She patted her ample thighs. "We have many, many children, me and you. You have camera? Come, take photo of us."

The bus broke down just in time. We stopped at a little roadside warung and I escaped from my prospective bride to the dimly lit interior. While the bus was being repaired, I had a meal of hard-boiled eggs and chillies, spiced by Satan himself. As I wiped the perspiration from my face and my stomach signalled its extreme disapproval, I took some comfort from the knowledge that soon I would be blowing some noxious gasses back at the smokers on the bus.

Back on board, the fattest woman in Sumatra sat down next to me. She had a child smelling of poo on her lap and it seemed as if she had tried to disguise her own sweaty odour with a lot of cheap deodorant. She was so large that there was no room for my rucksack on the floor between us and she stared at it sullenly, motioning for me to move it out of the way. Of course, there was nowhere else to put it and I ended up holding it on my lap. I started regretting my purchase of that large ceramic Buddha head, which was now painfully pushing into my groin. The fat lady squashed me against the window and I began to wish that the next person would take their turn to sit next to me, but it seemed that everybody had had a good look at me by that stage and that this lady and her pongy baby were going to be my close companions for the next few hours.

Then it started raining.

The window leaked.

The woman fell asleep on my shoulder and crushed me against the side of the bus that was now streaming with water. I got rained on from one side, drooled on by the kid and soaked with sweat by the woman. As if this wasn't enough, the cigarette smoke and the motion of the bus (manic bus driver as always) made me unbearably queasy. Gradually my legs became numb and soon I could no longer feel my feet.

When the bus broke down for the second time, I was very grateful for the chance to escape into the soaking rain. I don't know what was wrong, but the driver pulled into some kind of garage and spent two hours welding the front axle. After that the suffering continued; the fat lady did not leave me.

At 5 a.m. we stopped again. Relief! This time we had run out of petrol and someone hitched to the nearest town with a large container. Eventually we got going again until we reached a bridge that was so rickety that all the passengers had to get out and walk across before the bus could drive over it. We got back on and continued our journey, still stopping periodically to pick up and drop off more passengers.

I was not the only one on the bus that was feeling unwell. A few rows in front of us a man started vomiting and everyone crowded around him, apparently to see what he had brought up, as if it wasn't obvious enough from the smell that he had eaten some strong fish curry. Indonesians are the most curious people I know of. Then our afflicted fellow passenger threw a shopping bag full of vomit out of the window, splattering it along the side of the bus. Somewhere in the back a goat started bleating again. The driver kept on blaring his horn at every passing vehicle and he overtook the slower traffic wildly, almost exclusively on blind rises and hairpin bends. From time to time his head bobbed forward, as if he was nodding off, but he took several swigs from a bottle in a brown paper bag when this happened and this seemed to jolt him awake. From this point on I lost contact with reality, going through a sort of out of body experience. I wasn't completely aware of what was happening around me. My head slumped against the vibrating bus window and I felt my brain juddering around in my skull as I fell into fitful sleep.

Eighteen excruciating hours after the bus had set out from Parapat we eventually arrived in Bukittinggi. I didn't care what was happening anymore and I probably would have stayed on the bus for another eighteen hours, like a deluded hostage who falls in love with his kidnappers and refuses to go with his rescuers. But they dropped my surfboards onto the tarmac from the roof of the bus and that shook me out of my stupor. I leapt out of that bus and grabbed my board bag, cautiously inspecting the contents. Miraculously, there was no obvious damage to the boards.

Somebody handed me my rucksack and I staggered onto the road, feeling as if I had undergone some sort of religious conversion, or possibly that I had been brainwashed by the secret police to become a new man; a blank slate to start on afresh. I was a changed person: I had endured the Trans-Sumatran Highway and I swore that I would never ever in my life attempt anything like it again.

Chapter 1
Exploring Sumatra

"What makes travelling so appealing to me is that everything is renewed constantly. New challenges and different happenings arise all the time ..."

The reason for this trip through Sumatra's mountainous interior was, of course, to go surfing ...

Indonesia, the world's most populous Muslim country, is spread out over a huge tract of ocean, more than 5000 kilometres from east to west. That is greater than the distance between Seattle in the northwest of the USA and Miami in the southeast. Straddling the equator, Sumatra is Indonesia's western-most island and the fabled Mentawai Islands are spread out just off its coast, facing an almost endless stretch of the Indian Ocean. This archipelago was where I was heading. On most maps of this part of the world these little islands are represented by just a few small dots, but there are about seventy of them, some of them so small that they disappear at high tide, others large enough to support substantial towns and large expanses of rainforest. They are bathed in the warm, clear water of the strait that the local people call the Selat Mentawai and they are fringed by coral reefs with an inordinately high percentage of world-class waves breaking along their shores.

With lush tropical vegetation, brilliant white beaches and water in enough shades of blue to make any interior decorator green with envy, they are picture perfect. Swells that are generated in the ocean far to the south are groomed over thousands of sea miles until they meet the symmetrical reefs of the Mentawais to produce some of the world's best waves in a variety of locations amongst the islands. Now I was on my way to ride them.

But I did not want to merely fly in to the port from which I would be sailing. That would be boring. There were bound to be some interesting things in Sumatra's vast interior, with its varied peoples, its volcanic peaks and dense forests. Take for instance the Bataks, a group of fiercely independent tribes straight out of the Neolithic age, who had chopped off a good few missionaries' heads before they were eventually persuaded to adopt a more conventional (to us Westerners) lifestyle. I wanted to meet the descendants of these warriors and to see their country. It wouldn't be right to just sail around the edges of this massive island without at least taking a peak at its core.

What had set the ball rolling was a small advertisement in a surf magazine back home in South Africa: "Wanted: Six guys with guts". The ad was placed by Gerhard, a young attorney who had decided that surfing was more fun than suing people and that the solution to life's problems was to build a ship in Indonesia, sail it through this endless chain of islands and find perfect waves. The advertisement briefly outlined his idea and asked for volunteers with the will and the nerve to see through such an adventure.

In the end, what he really needed was six guys with money to fund his venture, but the whole idea appealed to me strongly. Like all other surfers, I had been reading about the countless perfect, deserted breaks in the islands. I had watched the videos featuring stoked professional surfers riding breath-taking barrels and living a dream existence here. As an expedition doctor, I had previously been to the forests of Borneo, Java and Sumatra and I knew a good adventure when I saw one. This opportunity was too good to pass up. I worked overtime and saved up money, while fantasizing about perfect waves, coral reefs and palm-fringed beaches.

Gerhard's grand plan had been to sail from Indonesia, through the Indian Ocean to the Seychelles and maybe even all the way home to South Africa. On the way he would surf, dive and explore the islands that lay between Africa and Asia. The journey would start in Sumatra, gateway to the Mentawai islands. The Mentawais had only become known as a surfers' paradise in the nineties. Some adventurous Australian surfers had been going there on surf trips for some years and slowly photos of wonderful waves in idyllic locations started to surface. The guys who were shown these sacred pics were probably sworn to secrecy, but of course stories of these places spread like wild fire. Soon the surf magazines were publishing articles about this fantastic area and every surfer wanted to go and experience it. But it was difficult to get to the islands and when we sailed in the year 2000, the Mentawais were still relatively un-crowded. Malaria and a complete lack of infrastructure kept travellers away. There had been virtually no development in this region and the surf charter industry was still fairly small. There were no surf camps and many surfers still hopped on local fishing boats to get to hidden surf spots.

From the Mentawais our ship would sail to Malaysia and Thailand, where perfect diving, full moon parties and exotic food would await us. Next, it would be a relatively short hop over to the Nicobar and Andaman Islands, some of the most isolated places in the world to be inhabited by humans. The people of these islands were not used to Westerners and not long before our trip some researchers had been attacked there with bows and arrows. The Andamans could have great waves on the right swell. Further west, India, Sri Lanka, the Maldives and the isolated Chagos Islands beckoned.

In order to make such a journey, Gerhard needed a good

ship. After investigating the different possibilities, he decided to build a traditional Pinisi, which is the kind of sailing ship the Bugis people of Sulawesi had been constructing for centuries. These sailors became the infamous pirates of the Malaccan straits, feared by all merchant ships. Apparently this is where the term "Boogie man" originated. So Gerhard, wife Charmaine and three other intrepid surfers went to the island of Sulawesi in the north of Indonesia to find someone who could build them a ship.

After two tries and a year and a half in Sulawesi, the right ship was eventually produced. It was a 120-foot ketch made of ironwood, with plenty of room on board, big fuel tanks for long-range travel and a powerful engine. She had a very shallow draft, about 2 meters if I remember correctly, so that she could navigate amongst shallow coral reefs. The vessel was painted white and she had the romantic look of a ship from a bygone era. She belonged amongst the islands of the East Indies and they named her the Island Explorer.

Often the best part of travelling is the preparation and anticipation before the trip. Getting all my equipment together was a thrill in itself. Nothing gets me as excited as taking out my mosquito net before a trip. The musty smell you shake out of it is like magic dust that takes over the senses. I was already seeing the forest and the beaches in front of me, feeling the warm water and gliding over untouched coral. This time I also had to bring extra surfboards, rash vests, and (gulp!) a surfing helmet.

But the major difference about leaving this time was that for the first time I had to leave someone behind. I had always been single when I had left on previous trips and there were only happy and exited farewells to envious friends and to my father who understood adventurous travel well. He had climbed South Africa's most interesting and challenging peaks at a time when mountaineering was considered eccentric at best and recklessly suicidal at worst. And he had dived some reefs on the

East Coast of Africa when diving masks were so scarce that he had to make his own out of an inner tube, a piece of glass and the rim of a Ricoffee tin. This all happened before I was born, but I had heard the stories and seen the photos and I had always dreamt of experiencing similar adventures.

A number of months after I had made the commitment to join the Island Explorer, I met Anne. A mutual friend had introduced us. The meeting place was a classy drinking establishment in Cape Town's trendy centre, but to make it more interesting we usually just say that we picked each other up in a bar. Anne was different from the girls I had met and gone out with before. She was a young attorney who had just completed her articles at a large Cape Town firm. Unlike most, she was in it for justice, not the money (she didn't stay a lawyer for very long; she's a psychologist now). She hated the sea, was terrified of waves, got panic attacks on mountains, disliked camping in basic conditions and didn't enjoy travelling to any destination that was unknown to her.

I couldn't resist her.

Of course I did not know anything about Anne on that first evening when we met, so I spent the night regaling her with stories of surfing, climbing and roving to the most unholy places. She kept a straight face through it all. And a few days later she asked me out on a proper date! It was a black tie function with lots of very superior people everywhere and I don't think that I fitted in very well with my blond ponytail, peeling nose and borrowed suit. But Anne and I got on like a house on fire.

Now I would be leaving her behind. We would be separated for at least five months if everything went to plan, with only e-mails from larger towns and occasional payphone connections through which to stay in contact. And if I entered really isolated areas, it would be weeks before Anne would hear from me. I knew that she would be worried and lonely; this time the thrill of walking through airport doors with surfboards and a backpack on my way to adventure was tempered by guilt and concern.

Despite all these mixed emotions, the feeling when I got off the plane in Sumatra was the same as it always is when I get off a flight in South East Asia. The humid, tropical air contrasts so strongly with the air-conditioned airplane that it feels as if you are getting a warm hug when you step onto the tar. You're instantly enfolded by the soft arms and ample bosom of the voluptuous (if slightly sweaty) beauty called Indonesia. At sea level Sumatra is hot, moist and fertile, with pungent smells everywhere. In Medan the sweet scent of flowers mingles with clove cigarette smoke and the more distant odour of open sewers. This fusion of aromas sums up the whole of Indonesia for me: natural beauty is everywhere and is so diverse, but it is un-sanitised; the place is real and unadorned. You won't be surprised by finding a lot of rubbish bins hidden in an alley around a corner. It's right there in the open for everyone to see. Not always pretty, but honest at least. And the fertility of the region helps nature to soften man's indiscretions. Even in the most built-up areas, plants force their way through the concrete to disguise some of the ugly constructions.

I have always liked to rough it while travelling. Shoestring travel forces you to really experience life on the ground in the area you are discovering, to get to know some local people and to find those magic places that package tourists never get an inkling of. The most interesting things happen when you have to live by your wits with only the help of the people you meet on the street. Sometimes you will get taken for a ride, but at least the ride should be an interesting one!

I dragged my board bag and rucksack away from the throng of clamouring taxi drivers outside the airport and loaded them into a tricycle becak (pronounced "beh-chuck"). You find this cross between a bicycle and a rickshaw all over Indo. It's cheap and flexible, able to stop anywhere, and it can go places where cars can't. Whereas it can be difficult to fit a bunch of surfboards into the average taxi, the becak driver simply lets them stick out at an angle and uses the protruding parts to keep pedestrians out of his way. The downside, of course, is that you are very vulnerable on open roads and Indonesian drivers aren't exactly subtle when it comes to overtaking. My driver pedalled into the kind of heaving traffic you find in most large third world cities. I'm always surprised by how these guys just glide between the oncoming cars and trucks and manage to survive. My driver crossed the lanes, negotiated the turns across oncoming traffic and avoided the cops (becaks which aren't motorized are slow and liable to hold up cars, so they were not allowed in the busy parts of the city) with a placid expression on his face. There was a Zen-like quality to him in the midst of all this hectic chaos; I never felt scared at all, even though there were some close calls with trucks whizzing past mere centimetres away. Some people trust in Fate to keep them safe on the roads. I trust in becak drivers.

I found the Sigura Gura hotel on a relatively quiet street not too far from some internet-cafés and moneychangers. It was a typical backpackers joint, with the usual mix of gap year students, overlanders and an older guy who decided to pack in his conventional job in Australia so he could find himself while travelling.

After sending Anne an e-mail to let her know that I had arrived safely, I hung around the lounge of the Sigura Gura. Here I met some German cyclists who were trying to cross Sumatra on two wheels. Unfortunately they had had so many close calls with trucks on the roads that they had decided to take a minibus out of the city into the countryside. Hopefully it would be safer to cycle from there. We agreed to share a lift and the next morning the five of us set out for the mountains to the south. After a three-hour ascent from the coastal plain into the mountains, we arrived in Berastagi. This mountain outpost is situated on the slopes of an active volcano, Gunung Sibayak. The Dutch colonists who came to Sumatra in the previous century established a comfortable base here. Its cooler climate suited their constitutions better and the incidence of malaria was lower at this altitude.

Berastagi is 1300 metres above sea level, so for a tropical town it actually gets quite cold at night. You need to sleep under blankets. After the hustle and bustle of Medan and the busy roads on my way there, Berastagi felt quiet and peaceful, a good place to rest up from the flight to Indonesia and to plan the rest of my overland journey. I decided to stay for a few days. The town centre consisted mostly of buildings from the colonial era, but there were also many traditional Sumatran long houses on the outskirts of town. These buildings have thatch roofs constructed in a saddle shape, rising at the ends of the house and making them look like the horns of a water buffalo from a distance. The walls are made of wood and usually the dwelling is raised on stilts. Often there were some chickens and a few dogs under the houses, with a vegetable garden in the back. Fruit trees like papaya, banana and mango were plentiful. The streets had virtually no traffic and I spent a pleasant day exploring the area on foot, looking at the architecture and being looked at by the local children, who were curious, but shy. Although people here had very few material possessions, they seemed content and there was no begging or hassling by the locals. The harshness of the city was absent and people had time for a quiet chat and a smile.

Over some steaming spiced tea that evening, the Germans invited me to tag along with them to the volcano. They wanted to climb it for the views and for the thrill of being on top of the world. We set off early the following morning, and it took us a day to climb to the rim and to peer into the smoky, sulphurous crater. Unlike most other volcanoes, the slopes of Gunung Sibayak were not very steep and there was a wide boulder-strewn rock field near the summit. In the direct sun we followed a winding path through the bare landscape and it was as if we were in a desert rather than in the tropics. But when I turned around and looked back, the almost fluorescent green of the jungle and the chaotic growth of trees, creepers and flowers leapt up at me from lower down, a vivid reminder of where I was.

Some people come to Sumatra for the sole purpose of climbing its volcanoes. These fiery peaks form a whole mountain range, the Bukit Barisan, spanning the length of the entire island, like the spine of a dragon with flaming breath. There are more than a hundred volcanoes, fifteen of which are active. The highest peak, Gunung Kerinchi, is 3085m high. Climbing them all could be an interesting project. I wonder how many people have managed that.

But cool air was not what I was really looking for in the tropics. I prefer the steaming forest floor and as I sat there on the rim of the crater, I was already making plans to move on. Next stop would be Lake Toba, the largest volcanic crater-lake in the world. According to geologists, the volcanic eruption that created it would have made Krakatoa's eruption (which sent smoke and ash halfway around the world) look like a little belch in comparison. Toba was a super-volcano and its eruption was on a completely different scale to any catastrophe that has occurred in human memory. This would have been the kind of eruption that could have pushed the dinosaurs into extinction. If it happened today, more than a billion people all over the world would die, there would be constant darkness for months because of the ash in the atmosphere and it would take years for our planet to return to a state of "normality". We were sitting right on the edge of the Ring of Fire, the chain of volcanic islands that stretches from Indonesia across the Pacific to the Americas and which periodically erupts into fountains of fire and rivers of lava. Sometimes entire islands are destroyed and new ones are created in the process, usually with devastating effect on us humans who get in the way.

"People are really insignificant on the face of this earth," Max mused as he peered at the spiralling smoke rising from the floor of the crater. "Look at how big this is. For all we know, it could erupt and vaporise us in a second. It is as if Mother Earth sometimes becomes irritated with us and burns off a few people here or blasts some others over there …"

That reminded me of something. "Do you remember The

Matrix? In that movie the machines said that humans have spread across the globe like a viral infestation, like a disease on the face of the earth. And they said that the planet had to be cured of us."

"Well, from that point of view, we're sitting in a dangerous place! Indonesia is definitely more geologically unstable than most areas."

"Yes, but the most interesting spots are always at least a little dangerous. I like that."

I arrived on the shore of Lake Toba just in time to catch a ferry to Samosir Island in the middle of the lake. With its blue water, lush and colourful vegetation and friendly people, this place could be paradise. In the sixties and seventies, Lake Toba was supposed to be the party capital of South East Asia. Hippies came from far and wide to zone out in the peaceful surroundings and to find themselves with the help of magic mushrooms, cannabis and other psychedelic aids. Apparently the full moon parties were legendary.

The first people who inhabited the area were the fearsome Bataks, who still using stone tools and practicing cannibalism when first encountered by Western explorers. For me as a South African, it was interesting that the parents of one of our well-known poets, the physician C. Louis Leipoldt, were missionaries amongst the Bataks more than a century before my visit. They did not stay for long, however, and Louis was born in South Africa. Converting Bataks to Christianity in those times must have been hell. The locals did not particularly like the Europeans and some missionaries were killed. A similar effort in the Mentawais by the German Missionary Society took fifteen years and one murdered missionary to produce its first convert. Leipoldt's mother was never happy in Sumatra and she could not get along with the other missionaries, whom she described as "a dishonest, lying & cheating set of hypocrites". She was constantly ill (probably malaria) and in 1879 they left for South Africa. One good thing Mrs. Leipoldt did achieve here was the initiation of schooling for Batak girls and women.

As a ship's doctor, Louis Leipoldt returned later in his life to visit Sumatra, or "Insulinde" as he called it, in 1912. Disappointingly, he did not write any poems about the surf or even comment on the waves. Maybe it was during a flat spell ...

Samosir Island had a slightly depressing air to it. It was clearly geared towards Western tourists, with curio stalls everywhere and desperate sellers looking at the few tourists appealingly and dropping their prices drastically to make a few Rupiah. Although it was five hundred kilometres away, conflict between government troops and hard-line Muslims in Aceh had scared off almost all the foreign visitors. The hotels and restaurants were empty and the streets were eerily quiet. When Leipoldt visited, he wrote about fighting between the people in Aceh and the then Dutch colonial government. They still haven't stopped, almost a century later.

It takes a few days of cycling to explore Samosir Island. There are secluded bays with small wooden cottages on the shores, overgrown with bougainvillea flowers and with frangipani trees beside them. Further inland, rice paddies and vegetable fields cover the landscape. Bright flowers grow in the fields and on the road verges. Early in the mornings I watched fishermen getting their nets ready and then heading out onto the lake for the day. Women washed clothes in the shallows near their houses and children played with the docile water buffaloes people keep as cattle here. It was an idyllic scene; you can see why the hippies liked it. There were still signs of the good old times on the island. Many houses had advertisements painted on the walls: "Have mushroom", "Get your good omelette here." But now the houses were run-down and people had a look of desperation in their eyes.

Not far from the main tourist town of Tuk-Tuk, there was a traditional Batak village consisting of ancient long houses, built in the distinctive local style, with soaring roofs and ornate woodcarvings on the walls. These homes have a grand appearance, unlike anything in the West and I was reminded once more that I was in a special place, far from home. There was a common area in the centre of the village, which was traditionally used for ceremonies, gatherings and executions. Apparently infidelity used to be a capital offence.

While I was talking to a man by the side of the road, a dog ran past, wagging its tail. Most dogs here are docile, of the smaller mongrel variety. The man noticed me looking at the dog and remarked, "That one is no good, it is the wrong colour." I asked why. "Black dogs taste better; we don't like the white ones so much."

On one or two evenings I joined some British gap year students for drinks, but they were trying too hard to have fun. The magic mushrooms, dope and booze were still available, but the carefree feeling of the hippy years wasn't there.

To pass some time and to try to improve my mood, I took the ferry to Parapat in search of an internet café. At least I would be able to converse with Anne, although the conversation would be very one sided. I looked around in the village, but unfortunately Parapat did not boast an internet café. I was told that the next town on, about half an hour's journey away by minibus taxi would have plenty of options. So I hopped in the cab that was pointed out to me and waited for it to fill up and go. My companion on the seat next to me could not speak much English, but as usual he was very friendly and very enthusiastic about teaching me Bahasa Indonesia. He pulled out one of those mini photo albums you used to get with your prints when you had some film developed and flipped through it, showing me pictures of his wife (unrecognisable because of full Muslim regalia, but looking petite under the black robe), seven children, many aunts, uncles, grandparents and others, all the while speaking to me very loudly, presumably to facilitate my understanding. Unfortunately this language lesson went right over my head and after increasing the volume of his voice until he was too hoarse to speak anymore, he gave up. Without further ado he put his arm around me, rested his head on my shoulder and fell asleep instantly, snoring loudly in my ear. I didn't quite know how to respond to this situation and I nervously glanced around me to see how other people viewed this new intimate relationship I had just become part of. I hoped that I didn't unknowingly agree to something he suggested while showing me the pictures of his family, but I was relieved to see that about half the passengers in the minibus were doing the same thing as my companion. They were fast asleep with their heads on a complete stranger's shoulder. (For the return journey I managed to get a seat next to a pretty young lady, but no dice.)

The little town I arrived at was typical of most Sumatran settlements. It was a hive of activity, noisy with scooters and motorbikes and full of people of all descriptions. Most of them were interested in me; clearly not many tourists came here.

There were buildings in different styles and sizes lining the streets, with jumbled wiring coming out of windows and roofs, converging on sagging telegraph poles. There were water stains on the walls from countless rainy seasons and the paint was peeling from window frames. From behind the windows and half-open curtains women peered at me and girls giggled shyly.

I avoided the touts and "friends" on the street and managed to get some young schoolboys to show me the way to an internet café. They were tidily dressed in uniforms of bright white shirts, neatly ironed grey trousers and shiny black shoes. They had friendly, open faces and sweet, respectful smiles and they were happy to walk with me and practice their English, making polite conversation.

We walked between puddles and around street vendors past a shiny, modern looking shop-front, lined with computer cubicles and with many customers working away in front of the screens. "Why not this one?" I wanted to know.

"No, no, they always kick us out when we look at porn!"

Writing a letter to Anne was very therapeutic. It enabled me to vent my feelings and by putting my thoughts down as words, I saw things in a more objective light. I realised that on the face of it, things were actually still pretty damn good here. I was living on a delightful tropical island, surrounded by friendly people, eating exotic food and relaxing all day long, yet I was not happy with my situation. It was time to stop complaining and to pull myself together. I resolved to change my attitude or to continue towards Bukittinggi.

Back on Samosir Island, I relaxed on the lakeshore by myself for a few days, reading, sleeping and cycling some more. But in the end I could not completely shake off the pervading air of despair. It was time to move on.

What makes travelling so appealing to me is that everything is renewed constantly. New challenges and different happenings arise all the time and bad experiences are usually easy to forget once you move on to another destination. You leave one place behind, get on a bus and arrive in a different world with a clean slate and high expectations. These days, with travel books, the internet and (still most importantly) word of mouth, you have a good idea of what to expect before you arrive. But sometimes there is a surprise; it doesn't matter whether it's good or bad. That special feeling you get when you look around you and realise that things aren't what you expected is addictive. This is the fix for the travel junkie; the constant curiosity about what lies at the end of this road or behind that rise needs to be satisfied. And when you find out what was hidden around the bend, you start wondering about what you would have found if you took a different direction back there. Could things have turned out better? You'll never know until you return one day. But I feel the compulsive traveller's approach to life, moving on constantly and in the process running away from his problems and responsibilities, can be problematic. Life can easily become a series of superficial encounters and I suppose the temptation to just keep moving away from commitments and mistakes will limit personal growth, ultimately creating an unfulfilling existence. Ralph Waldo Emerson said, "Travelling is a fools paradise ... I pack my trunk, embrace my friends, embark on the sea and at last wake up in Naples, and there besides me is the stern fact, the sad self, unrelenting, identical, that I fled from." Still, the freedom of travelling is like nothing else, but like the labels on beer cans say: Enjoy Responsibly!

I jumped on the ferry to Parapat and left Samosir and its air of quiet desperation behind in its wake. I felt invigorated by the change, as I headed for the bus station with a spring in my step. Good thing that I was well rested and that I did not know what the next eighteen hours had in store for me!

It was fairly early in the morning when I ended that marathon bus ride in Bukittinggi. I made my way over to the nearest losmen, collapsed on the first available bed and sank into oblivion. (I did not notice it at all at the time, but the name of my new lodgings was the Clean Achievement Losmen, which sounds like a very laudable name, but was not nearly as attractive as the Happy Love Losmen across the street. I wonder whether I wouldn't have been lured there if I were more awake at the time.)

Somebody rummaging through a rucksack close by woke me up in the late afternoon. His name was Ollie, he was from the UK (his village was called something like Crotch – how do the Brits manage to come up with these names?) and he was a laid-back, friendly bloke who was seeing how long he could stay in Sumatra before his money ran out. He had already made one visa run across the Straits to Singapore in order to extend his allotted tourist time in Indonesia by another three months. He liked mountaineering and the cool climate in the highlands suited him. He had struck a deal with our losmen owner and in return for sweeping the place, emptying out the rubbish and so forth he stayed for less, giving him an extra month of travelling if he was careful with his money. Our other roommate, Ben, also from the UK, was on the same money stretching program, but he had suffered a recent setback when a festive evening in one of the local bars turned into a bit of a party and he ended up spending several weeks' boarding money on beer. He had now gone tee-total (except if someone else was buying booze) and he was contemplating drastic measures such as giving up smoking pot and reducing his consumption of magic mushrooms in order to save some cash. We discussed his options while he was carefully splitting all his matches down the middle with his Swiss army knife, doubling his supply of lights. He gave me a look when I pointed out that he would not be using them much if he gave up the spliffs.

The fourth bunk in our room was occupied by Tom, who was a bit of a loner. No-one really knew who he was, where he came from or what he was doing in Bukittinggi. He would disappear during the days and only come into view in the evenings, when he would change his clothes and go for a meal at the warung across the street. He was an Apocalypse Now movie buff and he knew everything about it from start to finish. Recently Tom had arrived from Vietnam, where he had been retracing the movements of the characters in the film, travelling up unknown rivers into the wilderness for months. Tom could provide you with all the obscure details you didn't want to know about the film, from Marlon Brando's obesity problems, to Martin Sheen's heart attack, to the screenwriter's haemorrhoids. He did not seem interested in anything else in life. Tom always managed to steer any conversation he took part in so that he could bring "Apocalypse" into it. When that happened, the guys who already knew him quietly slipped away from the company. When he saw my surfboards, Tom immediately launched into an analysis of the scene in the film where the Americans attack a village in order to create a diversion while some of the soldiers go surfing. He knew all the dialogue too, right down to that dubious remark of the major to the hot young surfer in his platoon, "I've admired your nose riding for years. I like your cutback too ..." Tom made the whole scene sound even more like a pick-up line than it already did. I tried to explain to him that surfers just don't talk like that.

Hollywood doesn't understand surfing and so far, when real surfers have tried to make feature films, it's been disastrous too. Just check out In God's Hands, if you've forgotten. And I won't mention anything about the story line in Blue Crush. It will suffice to say that I don't think guys watched it for the plot or the dialogue. But no argument would change Tom's mind about surfers. Apocalypse Now was his reality and everything else was just entertainment. As far as he was concerned, all surfers walked around complementing each other on their style, and barked one-liners like "Charley don't surf!" intermittently.

Bukittinggi (meaning "High Hill") is perched on the slopes of the Minangkabau Highlands and the mountain air quickly revived me. I spent a few days exploring the surroundings with Ben and Ollie. Even though Bukittinggi is classified as a city, it has a small town feel to it and its centre, dominated by a quaint clock tower called Jam Gadang, was never too noisy or excessively busy. There was a pleasant town square, a remnant from colonial days when the Dutch had built a fort here and although we were less than a hundred kilometres from the hot and humid coast, the high elevation in the mountains meant that the weather was always relatively cool. The market in the town square provided everything we needed and was pleasant to stroll around in on an idle afternoon. The food was good and cheap here, with plenty of nasi goreng (spiced fried rice) and mie goreng (fried noodles). There were many backpacker-types around, creating a relaxed, alternative kind of atmosphere, a bit like being on a university campus, but without the exams. We'd sit around in the little restaurants that cater for tourists and we'd listen to blonde Scandinavians, the tall Dutch, serious Germans, flamboyant French and brash Australians discussing the local attractions and sights. The odd Canadian would be walking around with a maple leaf badge on their rucksack, so as not to be confused with a Yank. Usually, when we couldn't figure out where someone was from, they turned out to be Israeli. There were all sorts of people from across the globe, with divergent points of view, but we all tolerated each other and we got on well.

Normally I hate rain and gloomy weather, but I find that when I travel alone, bad weather has its advantages. I would sip a drink in a tearoom and before long a tropical downpour would drive a few other travellers indoors. It's easy to find people who share your interests in a place like Bukittinggi. After all, everyone goes there for more or less the same reasons. Some guy would take out a guidebook and start talking about where the best place is to catch the bus to the local market. Next thing we'd all be discussing the issue and off we'd go on another little adventure. As long as you're fairly flexible and open to new ideas, you'll end up having a good time.

Four of us visited Lake Maninjau, a nearby crater lake where the Minangkabau people live and we explored the local village, while getting soaked by tropical downpours every hour or so. We had not been there for long when we got more offers to marry some of the local beauties. The people here were friendly and they seemed genuinely interested in who we were, taking our visit to their home in the highlands as a complement. They gave us tea and rice and invited us into their houses.

As often happens in interesting countries, a local guide presented himself to us quite soon. Usually the guide is very friendly (at least initially) and he will show you all the sights, while telling you stories of varying accuracy about his town. Sometimes you can get by perfectly well without a guide, but there are places where you need them, like Marrakesh in Morocco. There you can get quite lost on your own in the more interesting parts of town. When you pass the stench of the local leather tannery for the fourth time on your way back to your hotel and the blind beggar on the corner starts to follow you discreetly, with a menacing expression on his face, you have to concede defeat and hire a guide to get you out, so you might as well have employed him from the start and gotten good value for your money. Agreeing on a price with your newfound friend before you set out is quite important too. By doing this you avoid the unpleasant situation on your arrival back at the hotel, when you realise that you don't have enough cash to pay the now exorbitant rate for his invaluable services and you end up having to hide in your room until after dark to avoid your now less than cordial guide.

On this occasion in Bukittinggi we met Mohamed, a self trained guide, who told us many stories about how the local people had to flee from the Japanese soldiers in the Second World War. Bukittinggi was the local headquarters of the Japanese during the war and they used prisoners of war and many local people to dig the Lubang Jepang, an extensive tunnel and cave system that extends around and underneath the city. Many people died while working deep underground. The locations of some of the tunnels were a very closely guarded secret and the story goes that in order to make sure that nobody disclosed their position, the workers who completed the most secret tunnels were buried inside them. Their remains were only discovered many years after the war. We were shown the wet, dark entrances of the tunnels leading underground, now blocked up or locked. I think I would have gone crazy, having to stay there for weeks on end, never seeing daylight and surviving on who knows what.

Mohammed agreed to show us the way up the local volcano the following day, so we went to bed early in preparation for the climb at dawn.

One great thing about Muslim towns is that you don't need an alarm in the morning. The call to prayer wakes you up just before first light. I find it easier to get out of bed in the dark when I know that everyone else in town is also up, doing their morning prayers. A quick curry breakfast ensured we were fully awake and we shared the local bus to the slopes of Mount Marapi with school kids and farmers on their way to the fields. The initial part of the ascent was fairly gradual, through rice paddies. We took the paths that the local labourers used to access their fields. It's hard to establish whom the land belongs to. Often people said that they were cultivating crops for themselves on land that did not belong just to them, so I suppose there was a kind of communal system.

As the sun began to rise, it became obvious that the volcano was enveloped in dense cloud. Already a fine misty rain was falling and it did not look as if we'd be able to gain the summit, something that I now think Mohamed was bargaining on. After an hour or so of walking around the rice fields, it became clear that Mohamed had no idea of how to get to the top of the mountain. I decided to at least try to get an idea of where to go, in case I got another chance to climb Gunung Marapi. We got directions from the men and women who tilled the slopes with hoes and shovels, going higher until we left the farmed land behind. Here it just rained harder and harder and at last we turned around and followed the streams of water down the slopes, craving the sweet tea at our local café.

Back at the losmen we could at least impress the other aspiring climbers with our comprehensive knowledge on how not to climb Marapi!

On my last day in Bukittinggi, I went to Sianok Canyon in search of the famous Rafflesia plant, which has the biggest flowers in the world and smells like rotting meat. (Strictly speaking, it's not a conventional flower; it's more like a parasitic fungus.) These blooms are bright red and yellow and are about a meter in diameter. The smell is there to attract flies for pollination, although going on the descriptions of those who have sniffed a Rafflesia, the odour might also summon some vultures and the odd hyena. (Un?)fortunately, Rafflesias don't flower very often and we didn't see or even get a whiff of one. Still, we had a great time crawling through the undergrowth, exploring the rain forest and thoroughly testing the waterproofing on our rain jackets. We did find some other interesting plants. The Mimosa pudica retracts and folds up its leaves when touched. I didn't know it at the time, but this plant greatly impressed Leipoldt during his visit. He described waves of motion rippling through the mimosa-covered slopes after he swept his walking stick through the bushes. Remember, he was a poet and therefore is allowed some poetic license. When I poked at them, they just pulled back their leaves rather timidly. Maybe it was just me, but they didn't wave.

It was almost time to board the Island Explorer, so with some apprehension after my previous journey, I went in search of a good bus to take me down the escarpment to the coastal city of Padang. This time I managed to check out the bus itself and to make sure that surfboards were allowed. It was a gleaming new coach with air-conditioning, plush seats and a television. The bus driver looked sober and professional and I felt confident that this journey would be a good one. Compared to the Trans-Sumatran Highway journey, this trip would be a short hop to the coast, just about a hundred kilometres or so. I was excited as I packed my bags for the next day's journey; it wasn't long before I would see the ship that would take me on a voyage to paradise.

Breakfast the next morning was a large ripe papaya that I still had left over from a visit to the market two days before. Then it was time to say goodbye to the guys I had become friends with and I carried my bags around the block to the bus station.

The coach was not overloaded and everyone had his or her own assigned place. I got a window seat and I settled in to take in the scenery as the driver pulled out of the bus station at exactly the right time. I was impressed. We moved slowly with the morning traffic until we came to the outskirts of Bukittinggi. In the distance, Mount Marapi was looming over the paddy fields, its summit enveloped in cloud as usual. Just when I expected the bus to start moving faster, we slowed down and turned off onto a gravel road leading up the mountain slopes. Soon it became a narrow track and we started bouncing over bumps and through potholes until we arrived at a little house where a woman collected some cash from the driver. I suppose he used part of the morning's fare to pay for something. Now that his personal affairs had been taken care of, I looked forward to the journey to Padang. But the bus did not turn back to the coast road. First we carried on up the muddy track to another house where a bag of carrots and some onions were handed to the driver. Next stop was at what looked suspiciously like a Muslim shebeen, where some boxes with bottles were loaded onto the seat next to the driver. After some inventive manoeuvring on the steep slope, with spinning wheels and lots of blue smoke, the coach was turned around and we headed back to the main route, stopping along the way to pick up some more groceries and a few plastic dolls. An hour after our departure time we were at last on our way again, the bus thoroughly covered in mud. It was around this time that I started feeling the effects of the papaya.

My digestive system made it clear to me that it was not happy with my choice of breakfast and that it was going to expel it shortly. Some nasty cramps started to take hold of my lower abdomen. Thankfully, I was on board a luxury coach and it had a toilet. I squeezed past the two other passengers in my row and hurried to the front of the bus, asking the driver's permission to use the loo (he had the key to the door). He wasn't happy to oblige, indicating that I would make a mess, ignorant Westerner that I was. But I knew that there was no way I could hold out until we reached Padang and I suppose he saw it in my eyes, because he gave me the key reluctantly.

Toilet cubicles on a bus are always cramped, but this being Indonesia, there had to be adequate washing facilities and so a large plastic container (almost a meter in diameter and filled to the brim with water) was placed in the only space available: right in front of the toilet where your legs normally go. If you wanted to sit down, you had to squeeze in next to the bucket, contort yourself to close the door behind your back and then climb over the sloshing water to get onto the seat, sitting with your legs in the air, as if you are at the gynaecologist. This is most undignified, especially when you have to do it all at very high speed because of the urgency of the situation. I made it just in time and as the relief of not having to clench for all I was worth came over me, I let my legs drop down ever so slightly. Just then the bus turned a corner and the water in the bucket splashed upwards, soaking my trousers completely. I sat there on the loo, leaning back with my legs in the air, dripping water everywhere and I wondered how far we still had to go and whether I could just stay in that cubicle until we arrived. The thought of squeezing past everybody with wet trousers was just too much for me. But there was no choice; someone was already knocking on the door. Now that the driver had allowed me in, everybody wanted to go.

The walk down the centre isle of the bus was awkward, to put it mildly. As I have said before, Indonesians are the most curious people that I have met and they all craned their necks to see exactly what was wrong with me, inspecting me critically and then having a general discussion about the state of my wet trousers and the possible causes. I sat down on my velvet seat without making eye contact with anybody and I watched the water soaking slowly into the plush cushioning. Not for long though. The papaya had not finished with me yet and soon I was squeezing past my fellow passengers again, on my way to the front of the bus, my ears blood red and my stomach contracting with an urgency that made me push to the front of the queue at the loo without even considering the outraged looks that I was getting. This time I didn't have to dip my legs to wet my trousers. The bus had started its descent of the mountain slopes and we were going through some tight switchbacks. The driver was not slowing down; he had a new coach and he was pushing it as fast as it could go around those bends, leaning on the hooter every time he neared one. As I sat on the loo, the water splashed onto my lap, over my shirt and ran down my legs. I emerged even wetter than before. The lady in the seat next to me looked at me as if to ask whether I was all right, but luckily she spoke no English and I just gave her a stupid smile and stared out of the window without noticing the scenery.

A few more visits to the toilet later we arrived in Padang. I never got off a bus so fast!

The air was hot and very humid in this port. Compared to Bukittinggi, this really felt like the tropics. Leipoldt's parents had stayed here before moving inland and at the time it seemed to have been a beautiful and unspoiled little town. His mother writes, "Those days in Padang will ever remain like an oasis in the desert of my memory." Unfortunately, Padang had rather changed since then. It was now grimy and smelly, with open drains on the road verges. They were big enough to fall into and disappear in forever and I made a mental note not to venture out after dark. The city centre was full of ugly, unfinished concrete buildings, interspersed with sterile modern blocks. Traffic roared everywhere and mopeds sped along between trucks and cars and on sidewalks. Just when you thought you had successfully negotiated the traffic in the road, a maniac on a scooter would come bearing down on you on the pavement. Houses had long since spilled over the city limits and built-up areas now sprawled over the surrounding hills that in the Leipoldts' time would have been covered with rippling Mimosas. Padang is the capital of West Sumatra and is Sumatra's third largest city. What a contrast to Bukittinggi.

Gerhard had recommended the Bumi Minang, the hotel that was used by most of the Westerners going on surf charters in the Mentawai islands, so I made my way over there. Cold air-conditioned air, fragranced with lavender, blasted my face as I walked in. The lobby was covered in shiny white tiles and there were mirrors and pictures in gold frames on the walls. Elevator music drifted around. A blond surfer was talking on a phone, telling the folks back home how big and perfect his waves had been. He kept confusing the Mentawais with the Philippines and he complained that clearly his Spanish lessons had been no good, because the locals never understood him. If his flight had been diverted and he had ended up in the South Pacific, I don't think he would have noticed. His friend was flipping through a surf magazine, while eating a McDonald's burger. We might as well have been in California.

I didn't like this sterile fridge and I went back to the hot street to find accommodation closer to what I had become used to.

A few blocks back from the Bumi, in an older part of town that had seen better days, but at least had some character, the Wisma Mayang Sari was more welcoming. Of course there was no air conditioning, the ceiling fan did not work, the toilets were of the squat variety with shower directly overhead (great for saving time by allowing you to do all your ablutions simultaneously) and the mattress had seen better days; but the general feel was relaxed and there was still a kind of dilapidated dignity to the joint. I did wonder about some of the other guests, who seemed to be mostly local businessmen – each with several pretty young wives. The wives seemed to come and go quite often; presumably they went shopping, because they were counting their money as they left …

I checked my e-mails at the local internet-café and there was one from Gerhard, confirming our meeting times and with some instructions on how to find the ship: "Just get a cab and tell the driver to take you to the 'kapal putih besar,' the big white ship."

A bearded Australian with a grey ponytail and a face lined with the imprint of many years of staring into the sun was sitting at the computer next to me. He wanted to know where I was headed. When I mentioned the Island Explorer, he said, "Oh, they have engine trouble, mate. They'll be stuck in port for the next few weeks at least. And that first mate of theirs, the big brawny Pom – he's completely bonkers. He might fool you at first, but wait until you get into open water, then you'll see! Better come with me, I still have one berth open and we're leaving tomorrow." At the time there were about fourteen charter boats working from Padang (now there are around forty) and competition for customers was already getting stiff. Because I had the e-mail confirming my itinerary open in front of me, I shrugged off his warning. I never gave it a second thought. "He's just looking for extra business," I said to myself.

I composed a long letter to Anne, because from now on there would be no regular communication with the outside world. I had no idea where we would be heading, except that we'd be sailing over large tracts of open ocean, sprinkled with little islands in places. Where our next port of call would be was anybody's guess.

On the way back to my hotel I stopped at one of several food stalls that open in the evenings. I was given a large serving of rice and then I could choose from a variety of barbecued meat, fish and vegetables on skewers. Everyone stands around eating at the food stalls and, although my ability to speak to the Indonesians was very limited, I enjoyed being part of this communal meal. Sometimes you don't have to talk. When I had finished eating, the skewers were counted and the price of my meal was calculated. This system was simple, easy and delicious – ideal fast food.

Chapter 2
Sea Legs

"In the aftermath of the wave I floated in the foam, checking whether everything on my body still worked and looking for blood in the water. Miraculously, I was fairly unscathed and so was my surfboard. Little by little, a sense of euphoria crept over me."

The following morning I loaded my bags into a taxi and made my way to the bay where the Island Explorer was anchored. I peered out of the window anxiously, looking for the kapal putih besar. As we came over a hill, I saw the white ketch for the first time, floating regally in the calm blue water. She really stood out from the other vessels in the bay, looking so grand that I started searching for another, less impressive ship. Surely I would not be lucky enough to go on that one! From where we were, the scene looked like a postcard from one of those places that I had always dreamed of when I was in some boring class at school. I was about to start living part of that dream now and it seemed completely surreal. The Explorer towered over the other boats and her traditional design drew the eye immediately. Her builders in Sulawesi had kept the design the same as that of all the old pirate ships of that region, but she was much bigger than the average Bugis vessel. The prow swooped up from the waterline in a great arc, with the bowsprit pointing up into the air. Two white masts rose from the deck, with brown sails tied closely against them. There was a spacious area in front of the wheelhouse, with additional space behind it in the stern, shaded by a canvass canopy. This ship looked like the real deal. Its size was reassuring in itself and the traditional appearance, with sturdy wooden planks and thick masts, made it look solid. It's the kind of vessel that people would instinctively trust; no doubt it would withstand a storm or two at sea.

On board I could make out some people sitting in the shade of some canvass, eyeing the shoreline. As I stood waiting on the little jetty, I had to keep reminding myself that here I was, in the middle of the tropics, looking at the ship that was going to take me on an adventure that had yet to be scripted and it wasn't all a dream. I didn't care about safety issues, engine specifications, or who the captain was. This was my ticket to discover places that no one knew about. I couldn't wait to feel the planks of the deck under my feet.

After a while a small motorboat came to take me to the ship.

Sean was the first person to meet me. Like me, he was from Cape Town and he was about my age. To earn a living he worked in IT, but he loved surfing and the sea. Of all the guests on board, he was the most experienced sailor, having crewed on a yacht in the Pacific a year previously. He had short reddish hair, thinning at the temples and although he was wearing only board shorts, drops of sweat had already formed on his forehead in the heat of the morning.

The Island Explorer was what advertisements and brochures would describe as "rustic". There was no air conditioning, no television and no satellite phone. Everything was kept to the bare minimum. I suppose your average package tourist would run a mile when they saw the facilities, but for me it was great. Everything was made of wood, with very little plastic or fibreglass. The deck was large enough to allow one person to separate themselves from the rest of the people on board if the need for solitude arose. The place to get some time to yourself was the bow, right in the front of the ship. This was where the anchors and cables lay. Importantly for us would-be sailors was the absence of a winch here; that meant that the anchor was lifted by manpower. An anchor big enough to hold a 120-foot ship is heavy. Soon we'd become very well acquainted with that anchor.

Toilet facilities are, of course, always a special issue, particularly for the ladies. The prettiest toilet I have ever seen was on a traditional Indonesian fishing vessel in Southern Sumatra. There was a simple screen for privacy and a neat oval shaped hole in the planks, jutting out over the water at the back of the boat, through which one could see deep down into the turquoise ocean with all its shades and textures. Around you there was the unlimited expanse of the Indian Ocean for a view. No artsy designer would ever come close, even in the best five star hotels. But, to get back to the Explorer's toilets: for a man there is naturally nothing more satisfying than directing a great arc over the side of the ship when nature calls. But when there is mixed company on board, other arrangements have to be made. The "heads" were of the traditional Western variety, but the flushing mechanism was different. There was a pipe connecting the outflow to the sea, but this had to stay closed at all times to prevent sea water from washing back through the pipe and flooding the toilets and the ship. When the ship was sailing and the movement of the vessel forced water into the pipes, one had to be very quick when flushing. This meant opening the valve to the outside fast, flushing a bucket of water down smartly and closing the valve again immediately. If you weren't quick enough, the backwash in the pipes would do an explosive reverse flush, sometimes with spectacular results! I know of one guy who had to shampoo his hair very thoroughly after an unfortunate toilet incident.

The cabins were basic, but spacious, with round portholes that could be opened to let in cool air on hot nights. We had wooden bunks, with comfortable mattresses. You could rig up a mosquito net over your bunk so that you weren't eaten alive when the ship was anchored close to land. Malaria was a constant worry.

Of all the surf charter boats, the Explorer was about the only one without air conditioning. Although there were nights when I wished for some cool air, I was glad that we weren't sailing around in some luxury yacht. This was the tropics and in the tropics it should be hot and sweaty. Cruising around in some artificial refrigerated bubble, only disembarking to surf perfect waves and afterwards dining on five star foods was not what I wanted to experience. I wanted to feel the Indian Ocean with everything in it and around it. I liked this no-frills, no-nonsense ship. It had an organic feel, from the creaking of the masts to the smell of the bilges and it seemed to have a connection to the ocean. Little did I know how soon I would be experiencing the real, raw Indian Ocean and the feeling an authentic Pinisi yacht can give ...

I shared the cabin right in the bow of the ship with Ron, a tall Kiwi. He had to bend almost double to get through some of the hatches on board. His height also complicated his surfing, forcing him to ride bigger, longer boards than the rest of us. Like most tall people I have met, he was an easy-going guy. He had a thick mop of dark curly hair and a Starsky and Hutch moustache. Ron had worked in many different fields, from big corporations in London to doing surfboard repairs for a shaper in the Pacific. He taught me how to fix my boards, an essential skill to master in these parts.

Back up on deck, I was shown the communal area in the stern. This was where meals were eaten when the weather was good and where everyone got together to relax with a beer or a cup of Java coffee. All the sunsets we saw from here would fill a movie theatre many times over. At the table, Pete was playing cards with Jonno and Esperanza. Pete was another doctor from South Africa. He had a perverted sense of humour and a sharp wit. No one could beat him at Scrabble. For some reason he liked walking around in a Speedo. You'd be out on deck on a sunny day and if you looked up, Pete would be half way up the main mast, wearing only his banana hammock, his eyes on the horizon and his mind no doubt in the gutter.

Jonno and Es were engaged. He was an Australian carpenter and she was a kindergarten teacher from Brazil. Jonno was by far the best surfer on board, having started surfing at the age of four and coming close to being a pro. The rest of us all thought he was good enough to compete on the world tour, but I suppose by some of our standards any good surfer looked like a pro. Es was a great body boarder and had a spontaneous, typically Latin temperament. When she got angry, you knew about it! From a surfer's point of view the great thing about their relationship was that their free time could always be spent in the water. There was none of the constant tension about surfing that so many surfers I know experience with their partners. No compromising on holidays; no sulky weekends spent pushing shopping trolleys around malls while your mates are surfing; no pacifying the wife on a windy beach after a three hour session. Jonno and Es went surfing on every holiday and it showed.

Then there was Francois, one of the original investors in the project, who had spent quite a bit of time in Sulawesi while construction of the ship was underway. With long blonde hair and tanned physique, Francois was easy going and he got along with everybody. He was always positive, even when the going was tough. He often walked around with a cockatoo on his shoulder. Seeing that the Island Explorer was modelled on a pirate ship, it was of course only right to have something resembling a parrot on board. Francois's bird was called Indie and she was allowed to roam around freely when we were out of range of land. Indie would flap around from post to post on the ship and she would occasionally have to be retrieved from the top of the rigging when she refused to come down. She had a mind of her own and a unique imagination. Every now and then we'd find a bird dropping in a place you would not dream a bird could get into and I think she left her calling cards there just to impress us.

A head popped out from the engine room and Gavin said "Hi". And I think "Hi" was all he said. Gavin was a man of few words and he preferred to keep himself busy working on the engine or the rigging rather than sitting around talking. He was a Cornish fisherman who Gerhard had recruited early on in the project. They had met each other while delivering yachts in the Med for rich owners. Gavin was big and muscular, like a diesel mechanic. He knew about ships and he knew about engines. Apart from trawling in the South West of England, he had worked on fishing vessels in the North Sea for a number of seasons and he was more knowledgeable about piloting ships than anyone else on board. Gavin had been present during the construction of the Explorer in Sulawesi and he knew her well. Gerhard had appointed him as First Mate of the ship.

During our introduction, Gavin kept fidgeting with a small water bottle, constantly screwing the cap on and off. He was clearly not very comfortable making small talk. I would soon notice that he never went anywhere without that water bottle. When he was working with both hands, he always put it down within easy reach and when he was at the helm of the ship, the bottle would be standing next to the wheel. It was always full and we hardly ever saw him drink from it, but our first mate rarely let it out of his sight. He was obviously fond of water.

Gavin was the only Brit on board. "So this is the crazy Pommie that the Australian from Padang was talking about," I said to myself.

Richard the cameraman was the last of the investors who was also crewing on the ship. He was older than the rest of us, in his forties. He had made a career in the film industry and the one story he told me that still sticks in my mind is about the time he had to film a live performance of the rock band Europe. They had a big hit in the late eighties called The Final Countdown. I think the concert was at a large venue in London and it was one of their biggest shows ever; the place was packed to capacity. The footage was going to be used to make the video for the hit single. There was a lot of pressure to get everything exactly right and a lot of money was involved. Richard is generally a very relaxed kind of guy, but the pressure obviously got to him, because he got the speed at which the camera was filming wrong and the whole performance was captured perfectly, except that it was all in slow motion! Remember, this was all in the pre-digital age, so it was impossible to change afterwards without losing a lot of picture quality. If you watch that video, you'll see that it has a hell of a lot of slow motion shots in it, with some other clips of different performances thrown in to break the monotony. I remembered that video well, I had taped it off the telly when I was a teenager and I had watched it repeatedly. After Richard told me about this incident, those endless close-ups in slow motion of the drummer banging away at his drums with sweat drops slowly flying in all directions and the lead singer's mouth gaping forever over the microphone made more sense. I think Richard started to work mostly outside of London after that episode ...

We spent another day anchored in the bay before all the supplies and passengers were aboard. Gerhard briefed us on safety. He showed us the life raft and the flares and explained the procedure to follow if somebody should fall overboard. There is a standard manoeuvre now for turning a ship around quickly. Basically the helmsman steers the ship in a special figure of eight under engine power in order to get back to the place where the individual went overboard. Even now, with fast, powerful motors, this takes a long time. Everybody on deck should keep his or her eyes fixed on the victim, because it is virtually impossible to spot a tiny bobbing head in an open expanse of water when you aren't sure where to search. In the old days of sailing ships, when it took ages to turn a vessel around, captains often did not even attempt to save a sailor who went overboard. It was just not possible to find anybody in a situation such as that. Every sailor knew that if he fell out of the rigging or slipped from the deck, that that would be the end. Apparently, many sailors purposely never learnt to swim so that they would drown quickly if this ever happened to them.

But we were not considering such a scenario. By this time we were all keen to leave the polluted water of the anchorage and to experience the idyllic islands we had seen so much of in magazines. So we weighed anchor and headed out on the blue ocean.

Consciousness came to me slowly and painfully. My head was hurting; I was nauseous as hell; my mouth tasted like snake spit and my back was killing me.

Daylight was just starting to filter through the closed shutters as I squinted through swollen eyelids to see what was going on around me. I was in the stern of the ship. There were two slim blondes, one on either side of me, each wearing only a bikini. I looked at them and felt better straight away. Richard was sprawled on the floor a short distance away, covered by a sarong. The shallow movements of his chest as he breathed were the only indication that he was alive. There were wet towels, magazines and various pieces of clothing scattered about the cabin and the four of us were lying in a mixture of water, food and vomit. I was, as Gerhard later put it, curled up in full survival position when he came into the cabin. He rummaged through the chaos and eventually retrieved his binoculars from underneath me. This cured my backache, but I kept my eyes shut tightly until he went away. I was still too miserable to contemplate facing the world. We must have had a hell of a party: no drink had ever made me feel this terrible before. By comparison, my worst hangover seemed like a spot of mild indigestion.

Slowly the events of the previous evening started to filter through to my throbbing brain, aided by some clues from my surroundings. There were no empty beer bottles or wine glasses lying around and no streamers draped over the furniture. This had not been one helluva New Year's Eve party; in fact, it was April and even though we were on board the most romantic looking ship in Padang, Richard and I had not been seducing the lovely ladies by candle light on the high seas. We had just experienced our first night on the Indian Ocean and it had not been fun at all. I turned over and retched.

I became gradually more disappointed as I recalled how I came to share a berth for a night with two sparsely dressed girls. Shortly after our departure from Padang, the Indian Ocean had welcomed us with a concentrated little storm. Out here they call these mini cyclones "Sumatran black eyes". You see the dark fist of clouds coming at you from the horizon and before you know it, it hits you hard, very hard. Rain pours down like it can only do in the tropics and the wind howls, first from one direction and minutes later from the opposite. These pocket-sized storms have given many an unsuspecting ship a severe battering and must have sunk quite a few over the years. To escape the weather, Gerhard decided to head for open water, away from the squall and from dangerous reefs. Often the storm passes quickly and it is over as suddenly as it had started – the sky clears, the winds die and all is peaceful again. But not that time.

We left the protection of the islands and found ourselves in an angry ocean with daylight fading fast. The water's surface had been churned into powerful waves, which were coming at the ship from various angles. Rain and sea spray soaked the ship and water started dripping into the cabins. In the galley crockery and cutlery slid around noisily in the cupboards. We were being lifted up and slammed down repeatedly by the waves. The ship rolled from side to side like a pig in mud and you had to really hang on to stay upright. We greenhorns weren't handling this very well. Soon almost all the new arrivals on board were seasick; we became a useless, apathetic bunch. The wind howled and the sea crashed onto the deck. The straining ship creaked and the struggling engine roared, creating an unearthly noise – the sound of doom. Through the murk in front of the wheelhouse I could make out Francois' outline, as he struggled around the deck, trying to save clothes and other items of value from being washed overboard. From where I was crouched down, I watched the bow of the ship gradually rise into the air as we struggled up an approaching wave and then suddenly dip towards the ocean floor again, as we lurched down into the trough between the swells. After every second or third wave another one would hit us side-on and everything that wasn't tied down would be flung into the air. The process repeated itself relentlessly, as if we had been abandoned on a funfair ride in hell. With each sickening downward dip, my stomach tore upwards into my chest. Acidic fluid collected in my gills and the most unbearable nausea took hold of me. Each movement of the ship sapped my energy and made me feel even worse than before.

Everybody who's been to sea knows the cliché about getting properly seasick for the first time: At first you feel so bad that you worry you might die; later on you worry that you might not. It's true. The only thing for me to do was to seek shelter and eventually I struggled into the cabin, where some of the others were already huddled together. Up at the helm Gerhard and Gavin were somehow managing to prevent the ship from sinking, keeping the bow facing more or less into the wind. I hunkered down as the ship floundered into the night, my stomach heaving uncontrollably until I passed out.

My mind was brought back to the present by another sideways lurch of the ship, followed by groans from my shipmates, so I got up and staggered onto the deck to look around. It didn't look good. Grey skies and choppy, broken swells made the ship sway, which made me nauseous all over again. Charmaine was roasting nuts for our breakfast muesli in the galley and the pungent smell hit me right in the gut. This was the start of a period of seasickness that lasted the entire trip. Whenever the sea was really rough, I would be hanging over the side of the ship and I never quite found my sea legs. The combined effects of my anti-malarial tablets, the grey day and my seasickness blackened my mood. I seriously questioned the wisdom of boarding the Island Explorer.

Considering the risks of going to sea off an exposed and very isolated coast with an inexperienced crew who mostly did not know each other at all, I'm surprised I wasn't more apprehensive in the first place. Our ship looked good on paper, but it turned out to be less than perfect on the open sea. Experienced sailors regarded her with a puzzled look on their faces. The masts were too short in relation to the hull and this made her difficult to sail. The shallow draught caused her to roll excessively in rough seas, upsetting even hardened seamen's constitutions. We ended up mostly using engine power when travelling, but this was another problem: the engine was slow and gave intermittent problems. She required constant attention.

Apart from the concerns about sailing on board the Explorer, there were worries about the deadly fighting between the Indonesian government and the fundamentalist Muslim separatists of the Aceh province in Northern Sumatra, the same unrest that had chased the tourists away from Lake Toba.

But this was before the Bali bombings and other international terrorist attacks on tourists had occurred and I never considered the possibility of such senseless killing by radicals. The catastrophic Boxing Day tsunami of 2004 had not yet hit the islands, nor had the earthquakes of 2005, 2009 and 2010.

Looking back on it now, it seems like we were heading straight for danger. I had met Gerhard only twice before leaving for Indonesia, but he managed to convince me that this trip was going to be a risk worth taking. A few minor problems did not deter Gerhard. He had a ship and he was going surfing with it, come hell or high water!

And so there we were ...

In the movies a storm is usually followed by a calm, sunny day. We weren't so lucky. The sea remained choppy and the skies overcast, bad weather for surfing and for diving. We found ourselves anchored off Pagai Utara (North Pagai), the island that was home to the famous surf spot, Macaronis. Apparently this spot was so named because macaroni was the only thing the first guys who surfed it had to eat. Alternatively, the slightly more bizarre theory is that it was named after someone had found a plate of macaroni on the beach shortly after an epic surf session here. Nothing to do with getting noodle arm from surfing the endless perfect waves, then.

It's easy to recognize Macaronis on surf videos and photos. There are some striking dead trees on the coast behind the perfectly breaking lefthander. It is definitely one of the must-surf waves in the Mentawais, but it wasn't giving us a chance on our first visit. The whole area was windblown and the swell was hitting the reef from the wrong direction. None of us knew the islands, so it was difficult to work out which spots to go to under these conditions. At the time of our journey, it was hard to get reliable information about surfing in the Mentawais if you did not know an insider. The Internet had yet to make an impact on surfing in these parts. There were no websites that mapped out surf spots and there was no Google Earth. We knew there was surf in the Mentawais, but we had to find most of the spots ourselves or discreetly follow other boats. Nobody was giving away any secrets.

Some years after we visited, a resort with all the trimmings was built at Macas. Speedboats ferried surfers from their luxury cabins on a crystal lagoon to the surf and back. In the evenings guests dined in a restaurant and could watch television, check the Internet and phone home to chat with the wife. If their muscles were stiff after a session, they could have an aromatherapy massage. But life here on the edge of a restless tectonic plate is unpredictable and dangerous. The earth's crust flexed its muscles and destroyed most of the resort in a few hours when huge seas followed a local submarine earthquake in 2010.

No doubt another resort will be built here soon and rich guests will be pampered once again – maybe a little further inland this time. There is money to be made from waves like these. But when we were in the area, there were no villas on a lagoon. Instead there was a swamp with clouds of mosquitoes and for a massage, the best you could do would have been to pay an Indonesian fisherman to walk up and down your spine to ease your backache. The only aromatherapy would be from his halitosis or possibly the smoke from the kretek cigarette butt hanging from the corner of his mouth. Still, we preferred it this way; the surf was often completely uncrowded.

But on this particular morning, Macas was not in the mood and Melissa and I decided to get into the sea kayak to escape the rocking of the ship and the queasiness it caused. Melissa was married to Derek, another doctor, who, like myself, had interrupted his career to go surfing. Derek persuaded his wife to learn to surf so that she would come along on this trip willingly, but his cunning plan was flawed. There wasn't enough time and Melissa was still practicing on a beginner's board and was not able to go near most of the reefs that we were going to surf. During the course of our voyage, Derek spent many hours doing romantic kayak excursions with Melissa while the rest of us went surfing cooking waves.

We paddled the kayak on the grey ocean, hitting the chop on the water side-on and struggling to maintain a rhythm. It didn't help that Melissa was a schoolteacher and that she kept on telling me how and when to paddle. We landed briefly on the beach, but there was no shelter from the wind and it was a cheerless place under these circumstances. After spending some time there kicking at little pieces of washed up coral and listlessly chucking stones into the sea, we headed back to the ship and hoisted the kayak back up on board, all the while bickering with each other. At least our short outing made me feel less nauseous and that evening I could enjoy Charmaine's curry and rice, made with local vegetables and spices. We didn't have a fully operational freezer on board, so no meat could be taken along and if we wanted fish, we would have to catch or spear it ourselves. When the sea was too rough to spearfish, we had to eat what was available from the larder. Later, when we were amongst uninhabited islands and the weather was bad, our menu was often rather predictable: noodles with canned tomato sauce and chillies.

The following morning we were all up early, hoping that the swell had been cleaned up over night and that we'd be able to go for our first surf at last . But the Selat Mentawai was still in a sulky, dark mood and she would give us no sunshine or waves. Gerhard decided to try his luck further south. Of course, going somewhere else always meant pulling up the anchor first. There were quite a few of us on board, so there were usually enough people on hand to do the job. About ten of us would stand in line on deck and heave on the anchor rope until it was aboard. Then Gerhard would put the engine in gear and we'd steam away slowly.

We usually cruised at about four or five knots, not exactly break-neck speed. One could sit on deck and take in the surroundings: there were countless islets covered with tropical rainforest and colourful birds soared above us against a backdrop of blue skies with cotton wool clouds. Everything looked just like the pictures in those brochures you page through while you wait for the travel agent to mix up your flights. The islands varied in size from just a few meters in diameter to several kilometres. Striking looking plants grew everywhere and only the white beaches were bare. From the deck I could make out ironwood, teak and strangler figs crowding lots of other trees on the shores. When the breeze blew in the right direction, the scent of the forest wafted over to us: spicy, exotic and elusive – a sensation on the edge of my memory; something I recalled vaguely, but couldn't pinpoint.

Sadly, a lot of the Mentawais' indigenous trees are being cut down for timber and to make way for palm plantations. A lot of diversity is being lost and many biologists who study these areas are concerned that plant and animal species still unknown to science are going extinct as their habitats are being destroyed.

Many of the tiny islands are uninhabited, but people own palm trees on the land and they come to harvest coconuts periodically. We would sometimes see them camping under the trees, with their harvest in a large heap next to their sleeping shelter, which they build within minutes. It's amazing to watch a skilled person work with a parang (machete). The builder chooses some young trees of about the thickness of a man's forearm and chops them down with a few quick blows. Then he clears them of branches and plants these poles in the ground. Next, more trunks are lashed horizontally to the posts, using strips of bark as rope. The roof is constructed by putting smaller branches and large leaves on top of the shelter. The frame of the shelter will still be there when it's time for the next harvest and one only needs to add some leaves to make the roof watertight again. Finally, some leaves from a special shrub are used on the ground as sleeping mats. These not only keep the occupants of the shelter off the damp earth, but also seem to have a mosquito repellent action. All the building materials grow right where they are needed and no supplies need to be taken along. The rain forest is so crowded with plants that there is never any shortage.

Watching the harvesting of coconuts is best done from a safe distance. These guys have clearly been climbing coconut trees since early childhood and they shimmy up the trunks very fast. Soon after they reach the branches the coconuts start crashing down and if you happen to be standing underneath the trees, you'd better be very agile if you want to avoid getting brained by one. Remember that often quoted statistic about more people being killed by falling coconuts every year than by car crashes, serial killers or whatever catastrophe you prefer? You can see where the idea comes from.

By now I have climbed many coconut trees, but I choose the trees that I climb carefully and I stay relatively close to the ground, just high enough to get to the lowest coconut. The locals here climb a few stories high and hardly even bother to hold on with their hands.

We arrived at our next destination, a few tiny islands grouped close together, providing more shelter than our previous anchorage. The swell was wrapping around a coral outcrop and it formed a small, relatively clean wave, just about surfable. We were so desperate for waves by now that quite a few of us paddled out into the lukewarm sea and we managed a few rides. They certainly weren't memorable in themselves and I don't think this was even a recognized surf spot, but it was my first surf in the Mentawais. We sat on our boards in the middle of nowhere, staring at the nearby jungle with its empty shore and we wondered whether anybody had surfed here before. There were no local people to tell us. For all we knew this spot became world-class on a bigger swell; then again, maybe this mediocre wave was the best that this spot could deliver. There must be thousands of similar set-ups in this island chain and the surfing potential is endless. Yet most surfers who visit the Mentawais head straight for the famous, crowded spots and fight for waves there with throngs of other surf-crazed tourists, generating more of the stress that they were trying to escape from when they came here in the first place.

I paddled back to the ship feeling good. It felt like ages since my last surf back at home and I had really enjoyed being back in the water. Of course, the waves were nothing special, but the idyllic setting, the bright coral under the surface, the bath-like water temperature and the relief of being free from the seasickness of the previous days had made the session great. Jonno and Esperanza were sitting on deck; they hadn't bothered to paddle out in these waves. As I came on board, Es asked me how long I had been surfing. She wasn't one to delicately phrase questions in order to spare people's feelings and she didn't look very impressed by my talents! I had started surfing relatively late in life, when I was twenty. Many people who start behind schedule like this never progress beyond surfing easy beach breaks on a Sunday afternoon. To become a truly proficient surfer, you need to learn when you are young enough to imprint the basic techniques in your brain so that you can surf on instinct, without thinking. My saving grace is that my father had taught me to bodysurf as a young kid and from there I had started riding body boards. This gave me a feel for the wave, making it easier to learn to surf standing up when riding a sponge became boring. Nevertheless, medical school and hospital work had demanded a lot of time from me and I suppose that all work and no play can make Jack a dull surfer. Still, although I was very aware that I was never going to become the next Shaun Tomson, I did feel that I could ride waves without causing serious injury to myself or to others.

But Es' remarks had left me unsure of what was going to be required of me in Sumatran surf. When I had taken the decision to come on this trip, I never considered the possibility that I could find myself out of my depth in the water. Watching video footage of the world's best surfers pulling into tubes here and making it look so easy fooled me about the degree of skill required to master the reef passes of these islands. I didn't realize that the stars of the videos were obsessed with surfing and that they were ridiculously talented. They made it look like a walk in the park. In my mind I simply inserted myself in the place of the poster boy standing casually in a translucent barrel, dragging my hand along the surface of that fantasy wave and smiling for the camera. For some reason I just assumed that if I were in an idyllic location such as the Mentawais, I would be able to ride tubes effortlessly, unlike back home where barrels were elusive and successfully riding them was even more so. I think the relative isolation (from a surfing point of view) of the inland town where I grew up, limited contact with good surfers and a belief that I would easily achieve whatever it was that I attempted, made me naively think that I would simply be able to handle any situation in the water. After all, thus far I had always been ok everywhere I had paddled out, even when some other guys got scared. I was like Rick Kane in the movie North Shore: a small fish from a small pond, and I was blissfully unaware that, unlike in the movie, it takes a long time to improve your abilities to the level of handling heaving reef waves. It would not be long until I was made very aware of this...

We decided to sail on again, looking for Thunders, a surf spot on an island further south. Gerhard had been given some information about its location, but we were unsure about where exactly to find it. We squinted at the vague pencil marks on our nautical map in the wheelhouse and Gavin set a course for a likely group of islands. After an hour or two, we spotted some greenery on the horizon and as we studied the hazy outline of a small island with binoculars, we could make out smoke rising vertically into the air. This was a good sign. Firstly, it meant that there were people living on the island, making the likelihood of this being the place that we were looking for greater. Secondly, the vertically rising smoke column meant that there was no wind – ideal conditions for surfing. Gavin pushed the engine a little harder and we craned our necks, peering at the island in anticipation. As we came closer to the little green patch with its white ring of sand around it, we knew we were in the right place. We could make out another yacht lying in the channel between two small islands. Those aboard it were bound to be surfers.

The Explorer moved in between the islands and we were confronted by our first perfect Mentawai surf set-up. It looked exactly like those photos in surf magazines that had lured all of us halfway around the world. I think this kind of picture will always remain almost every surfer's fantasy, the image that motivates us all to paddle out in the cold and the rain, in howling onshore conditions when we would rather be doing something else. Because one day we hope to arrive at a destination such as this and when we do we want to be ready for it. The turquoise water in front of us was smooth and clear, with clean swells moving along the surface, lifting our ship up and down gently and rhythmically. Along the shore of the island, we could see white lines running over a reef for about a hundred and fifty meters until they reached the shallows. There was an endless supply of evenly spaced waves following each other, bending and refracting around the island, curving along the shape of the coastline. Across the channel on the smaller island a mirror image was unwinding along the reef on that side; the break was not as perfect, but with more punch and power. From close by we could see the waves there lurching and spitting, interrupted occasionally by a section that would make it difficult to ride it successfully on this tide. We had found Thunders and Rags. Waves that break from left to right when you face them are called lefts and their mirror images are rights. Thunders is a left and Rags is a right. The boat that we had spotted earlier was anchored between the islands, close to Thunders and we could see two guys sitting on deck, watching their mates in the water. The waves were shoulder to head-high and the sun had just appeared from behind the clouds. There was not a breath of wind and the surface of the water was perfectly glassy; not a ripple could be seen on the wave faces. They were hollow without being too intimidating and there were barrelling sections as well as open faces to carve.

Five surfers were enjoying the ideal conditions, moving up and down on the blue walls, weaving along, sometimes carving gradual arcs and at other times doing sharp snaps. They were having a ball. Boat etiquette required that we wait a while before we joined them. There were ten surfers on our ship and if we all jumped in the water, it would spoil the session for the guys who were on it first. There wouldn't be enough waves for everyone. Resisting the temptation to head over to Rags and its less perfect waves across the channel, we sat down to a meal of tinned sardines and crackers, eyeing the enticing surf and marvelling at our surroundings. After lunch we headed out.

Thunders, despite its name, is one of the less intimidating waves in the area. Maybe it was named because there was a thunderstorm nearby when it was first surfed, rather than for the thundering waves. This is not to say that the spot doesn't get heavy when the swell jacks. A while later we had a serious session there in big waves. But this first session did not go well for me. In spite of the great conditions, I kept on messing up my take-offs; I either fell immediately, or I was so off balance that I just flapped along on the wave, out of control. I started losing confidence and this caused me to make more mistakes. As I paddled back from yet another frustrating ride, a bigger set started breaking on the reef and instead of being able to paddle around the waves I had to duck under them. The white water bearing down on me formed a high foaming wall and to escape this I instinctively pushed my board as deep under water as I could. The next moment I felt fibreglass splinter as I drove my board into the reef. My first lesson in the Mentawais had been that the sea could be rough. The second lesson was that the reefs were shallow, very shallow.

That evening I tried to console myself with the thought that at least I did not get hurt on the reef. My surfboard had taken the punishment for me and the damage could be repaired. Over the coming weeks board repair would be a skill that I would be honing to a fine art.

While we had been surfing, Gavin had gone spear fishing and he managed to get a large trevally, a very tasty game fish. Es was admiring Gavin's catch.

"How long do you have to hold your breath to find a big fish like this, Gaveen? Ooh, it musta be such a thrill to follow it under water and then to get it eventually! Does it drag you around after you shoot it? What happens if you run out of breath? Were there lots of other fish or did you have to look hard to find this one? You must be very proud of shooting such a wonderful fish!"

"Err, I was just trying to find something for supper," Gavin was taking the cap off his water bottle and screwing it back on rapidly, looking at the fish uncomfortably.

"Are they very fierce? I mean the fish?"

"No, if you hit them in the right place they die quickly."

"And what about the teeth ..." But Gavin had picked up the trevally and was walking to the galley, leaving Es a little confused. She wasn't used to being left behind in mid sentence.

Whenever the conditions allowed, we ate fresh fish. It was rare that one of the spear-fishermen went out and did not return with enough fish for everyone on board. On a few occasions in certain areas we did see signs of dynamite fishing, with large areas of lifeless reef, devoid of any coral or marine creatures. These islands are so remote that they are impossible to police and a few individuals can easily get away with this ignorant practice. Luckily, we did not see too much of this kind of destruction.

It's amazing how a good meal can improve one's mood. Over supper it was decided to steam overnight to an area called The Playgrounds. Filled with grilled fish and some Bintang beer, I was looking forward again to my next surf. Overnight we travelled northwards towards Sipura Island.

The Playgrounds is probably the closest a surfer can come to paradise. A group of islands form a semicircle, with perfect waves breaking along most of them. Would you like to whack a few fun walls? Feel free. Or do you fancy pulling into some spinning tubes? Just help yourself. Everything is right there for you. The waves vary in intensity and quality; on the more exposed reefs you can get your adrenalin rush and later on you can paddle out at one of the more protected spots and have a more mellow session in beautiful surroundings. The islands themselves are lush with trees and they have brilliant white beaches. When you are tired of surfing, you can rest on the coral sand or lose yourself amongst the trees on the islands.

Shortly after we had been here, an international surfing contest was held in the area, but after some days in the vicinity, the professional surfers went on strike, saying that the surf was not challenging enough and that the perfect waves were making the contest boring. In response the contest was moved around the corner to Kandui, one of the fastest and shallowest lefthanders you'll ever surf. In fact, it's a wave that many of us would rather stay away from. When you take off on this hundred-metre stretch of fear and trepidation, you either go straight to heaven (if you make the wave) or to hell (if you don't), with no middle ground. Usually you visit both places in one session. If you are good, Kandui will give you the deepest tube rides of your life and you'll have verbal diarrhoea about the experience for decades. But at some stage or another it will demand payment in the form of flesh. Kandui is nobody's friend and it will rake your body over its jagged reef when you make even the smallest mistake.

Most of the participants in that contest broke a few boards and quite a few got some reef tattoos during their sessions, but the challenge of riding these speeding tubes was what they had been looking for and they ended the competition feeling stoked and fulfilled, gushing about their experiences.

However, when we checked it out, I did not even remotely consider Kandui a surfable prospect. I simply stared at the frothing, foaming fiends that lurched across the reef and when some of the boys said they were paddling out there, I almost peed in my boardshorts and slinked below deck for a spell. Remember, at that time nobody we spoke to had heard of it being surfed before. Lured by the perfect, spitting barrels, Johnno, Gerhard and Sean braved the water. They sat in the line-up and paddled for some waves, but time and again they pulled out in the last instant at the sight of raw coral waiting directly below them. When they returned, the consensus was that it wasn't a make-able wave. It took some pros to show what was possible here and now it's a sought after surf spot. Maybe we were there when the tide was too low or perhaps the boys were just chicken. I certainly was and I don't think I would have survived Kandui on that day.

Happily for us, there were plenty of alternatives to surf in the area. Nowadays there are a number of surf camps at The Playgrounds and I think that the spots will always be crowded in season. All the charter boats also do a regular milk run here, but on our first morning, we motored out to Rifles and had it to ourselves. You can see why the spot is called Rifles; it fires! The waves were flawless. Clean and fast, with almond shaped tubes and long walls to race along, it was hard to make a mistake, but somehow I managed to mess up every one I caught. Some of the boys got some deep barrels and I paddled into several waves with high expectations, but every time, when I was on a critical section, something went wrong. I dug my rail, fluffed my turns and I fell time and again. Back on board ship we had breakfast with the late risers and we watched some super motivated Japanese surfers ripping up the nearby inside wave. After they had exhausted themselves, I decided to paddle out there to regain my confidence in less intimidating conditions. I had a few waves, but the swell seemed to be on the wane and a dropping tide took the power out of the surf. Instead of kicking out of my last wave as usual, I let my board sink into the water under my weight and bingo! I hit the reef again and was left with a hole in my second board.

That night in my bunk I dealt with the angst of realizing that I was in surfing heaven, but that somehow I was unable to surf properly. It was like being a eunuch in a harem: all these beautiful waves everywhere, but I couldn't do any of them justice. After fantasizing about being in a place like this for years, saving up to afford it and then travelling through grimy cities, overgrown roads and surviving crazy bus rides, it was a bit much to accept. I had to admit to myself that I was surfing like a kook. Calling a surfer a kook is probably the worst insult possible. A kook is someone who doesn't understand the essence of surfing. He can't really surf, but he thinks he can. His style sucks; he can't do proper manoeuvres; he falls a lot and generally just looks shit on a wave. And I fitted that description. I shuddered at the thought of what I must have looked like over the past days.

This situation had to change. Once I had accepted that my surfing was basically kak, I could do something about it. I knew that I had surfed similar waves at home successfully. I had at least some ability, but I needed to change my approach;

basically I had to learn to surf all over again and to adapt to the more challenging conditions. These waves were faster, much more hollow and way more dangerous than your average beach break, but not impossible to master. I had to get my mind right first, master the basics and build up my surfing again. One thing that counted in my favour was that I was fit. Learning to surf in Cape Town might not have prepared me for tropical reefs and tricky barrels, but it did teach me how to paddle. Most of the surf spots that I frequented had no convenient rips or piers to jump off in order to get to the waves. Endless paddling and duckdiving under set after set of churning white water had trained my shoulder and arm muscles and my lungs were in peak condition. This gave me confidence.

I felt more positive after having made a conscious decision to address my problem and as I turned over in my bunk to go to sleep, I felt a little more hopeful.

As I lay there in the dark, sleep wouldn't come and I thought again about how and why I had landed up on this ship in such an incredible location. What had kept me going through medical school, my internship and 120-hour workweeks in chaotic hospitals while bordering on delirium from lack of sleep, was the thought that one day I would be able to use my qualification to come to a place like this. For a while I had become side tracked, like a religious zealot who is lured away by a false god. I took up mountaineering and climbing in a big way. My friends were climbers, not surfers.

When I was a student in Cape Town, every Friday evening I would take the train from near the medical school where I was based and ride to Stellenbosch. (We medical students had been banished from the revelry at the Stellenbosch University campus to the wastelands of Parow Valley and the huge hulk of Tygerberg Hospital.) On those Friday nights I would walk to a pub where I would meet my friends and then we would talk all night before setting off for the mountains at dawn. We spent our weekends exploring the nearby crags and peaks and during varsity breaks we would venture further inland, to more challenging places, far away from the sea. We slept high up, close to the stars, night after night. Water was for drinking only or maybe for a quick dip in a mountain stream. But we didn't allow ourselves to be slowed down on our way up, up and away, always further from the coast and from the ocean. I joined the Mountain Club, I read climbing magazines and I did pull-ups by the tips of my fingers from the narrow ledge above my doorframe. I was as fit as any of the top mountaineers. And I developed a farmer's tan.

But I never quite forgot the sea. My parents had managed to buy an ancient little Datsun for me; it was a light brown, mustard coloured car. My father said it was the colour of baby shit and now that I have my own boy, I can confirm that he was right. The reasoning behind buying the car was that, as I was progressing through the medical curriculum, I was beginning to work longer hours at the hospital at irregular times, often until late at night. I needed my own transport. And naturally I agreed wholeheartedly with my parents.

Of course I knew that the real application of the car would be to go surfing. On weekday mornings I would endure the syrupy love songs and romantic ballads on the local radio station so that I didn't miss the surf report at a quarter past seven. And if the report sounded good, class wasn't an option. I would jump into that jalopy with my surfboard on the folded down passenger seat next to me, gun the engine and drive in my baby shit coloured streak all the way to the beach twenty five kilometers away.

The fickle waves on the stretch of coast between Table View and Melkbosstrand, just north of Cape Town, became my training ground. Usually, I went alone, pushing under the icy water while horse riders from a stable across the coast road galloped past on the beach, oblivious to me and my solitary quest to learn to ride waves. I preferred the lonely breaks to busy spots because I was embarrassed to be a beginner at my age. I resolved to get good first before going to the popular places, where kids half my age were ripping up the surf. Unfortunately, this attitude slowed my learning a lot; watching experienced surfers is essential for acquiring vital skills. And often a break is uncrowded because the waves are poor there on that day, limiting one's opportunities to practice. Luckily, I started to make friends who surfed and on some occasions they dragged me along to the better-known breaks.

To kill time between classes or just as a diversion from studying, I would go to a local book store and read the magazines on the shelves. Gradually, I found myself drifting over from the climbing section to the surfing mags. The pendulum was beginning to swing away from the mountains, in the direction of the ocean again and I was steadily brought back to the religion of the sea.

As time wore on, I started cutting the time between surf sessions and ward rounds very fine. I would surf until the very last minute, run up the beach to my car, rip off my wetsuit and get dressed while waiting at traffic lights on the way back to the hospital. I would rush into the ward just in time and tag onto the back of the group of students as they walked from bed to bed. Once, when I bent over a patient to examine her, salt water drained from my sinuses and ran out onto the bedding. Our tutor looked at me critically and remarked, "Really Scheffler, you seem to have a cold every time we have a ward round. Look at how red your eyes are; you seem exhausted. You should take a break from studying every now and then, you know. Go to the beach or something, it will do you good!"

Believe it or not, I actually did work very hard at my studies and I did pass every year fairly comfortably. I learned how to manage my time efficiently: when the surf was no good, I studied non-stop; when there were waves, I surfed as much as possible. This became more and more difficult as we started spending more time in hospital and less time attending classes. But surfing became a refuge for me, a crutch. When I got bad marks for a test, I surfed to ease the disappointment. When a girl turned me down, I went to the beach to alleviate the pain. My mother was terminally ill at this time. When I was younger, she had always been the person whom I turned to for support when life got hard. Now her illness was the main cause for my distress and I could not unburden myself with her. Salt water and the rocking motion of the deep became my substitutes.

Eventually, our class graduated and a group of us went on to do our practical year in, of all places, Windhoek. Windhoek is a small city in the middle of the desert four hundred kilometers from the coast in Namibia. I didn't surf a whole lot that year.

Instead I subscribed to the Zigzag, the only affordable surf mag in the country at that time, wrote hopeful letters to surf resorts in the Maldives (which went unanswered), and swam endless lengths in the brown-green water of the swimming pool at the intern's residence. The following year financial considerations sent me across the Atlantic to the place all South African graduates with a study loan seem to end up in: Great Britain. Actually the Mud Island doesn't sound all that bad to a surfer. After all, it's surrounded by waves. Scotland has some of the best surf in the world if you can stand the cold and then there is Northern Ireland, with endless potential. Further to the south, on some summer days, Cornwall can look like Biarritz. Well, almost.

But I ended up in Stockport.

Don't ask how; it's a long, sad story. Stockport is the pimple on the arse end of Manchester. The abode of football hooligans and lager louts, this is where yobs go to feel at home. It looks like the set for Coronation Street and it's probably the only place in the world where sane people address each other as "Duck", as in "Fancy a pint of lager, Duck?"

And my job was in psychiatry.

The closest surf is about three hour's drive away in North Wales, not the most consistent place for waves. Factor in weekend traffic and you can easily drive five long hours for the pleasure of surfing freezing knee high dribble. And then you have to drive back again.

On one Friday evening after months of never seeing the sun and no surf at all, I walked past a billboard advertising holidays in Mauritius. There was a drab black and white picture of a man in a gray coat and umbrella standing in the rain. The caption was "Man Thursday" (Manchester Thursday, geddit?). Next to it was a full colour picture of the same man looking relaxed and tanned, sitting under a beach umbrella, holding a cocktail. This one was titled "Man Friday" (Robinson Crusoe, wasn't it?). It was then that the absolute awfulness of my situation hit me and I nearly started crying there in the street, while all the sallow, pale faced people who were queuing for fish and chips on the corner stared at me. But that was the catalyst I needed to get me out of there.

Not long after that Friday I found what I needed in the careers section of The British Medical Journal: an expedition to the forests of Sumatra required a doctor's services. You needed to be fit and the work would be unpaid, but it was for a good cause, research on the endangered Sumatran tiger. I jumped on the train to London for the job interview and made damn sure that I said all the right things to get the position. Maybe my working experience in Africa impressed him, or possibly the expedition leader saw that I was on the verge of cracking and that I would assault him if he turned me down, but he gave me the job and I was over the moon.

Before I left Stockport, I went to take a picture of the billboard that had made such an impression on me. I still have it.

That was the start of my love affair with Indonesia. I returned there after my first visit, again as an expedition doctor. We went deep into the jungles and high up the slopes of volcanoes, but rarely to the coast. There was always something that prevented me from going surfing after the expedition ended; circumstances conspired to keep me from getting to the waves. But on one occasion I had glimpsed perfection.

We had just completed a long stint of working in the rainforest in South Sumatra. After two months in the jungle, the leeches, snakes and scorpions that we were so nervous about at first had become almost a routine nuisance and we no longer noticed the constant dampness of our clothes from the daily rainstorms. Mould grew on our clothes, on our backpacks and in our shoes. Our only deodorant was DEET spray and our dreams were Lariam flavoured.

The two-day walk back to the coast had finally cured me of any remaining affection for the word "feral", so often used in surf films and exotic advertisements. The beach, with its dry sand, clear water and direct sun was a luxury. Clean, three-foot waves fell on the sand and washed over my feet.

I dropped my backpack on the beach and flopped down into the warm water to let the waves wash me around. After the sweat and grime had gone, I walked back up the white sand and sat down in the shade with the rest of our group. We decided to sleep there that night and to complete the walk to our pickup point the next day.

No tourists ever came to this coast and charter boats didn't venture this far either. Local people had no reason to come here. This beach was as isolated as any beach in Sumatra.

A rickety old jetty, sun bleached and warped with time, was the only evidence that humans had ever come here: loggers, after stripping the land of useful trees and shipping them away had abandoned it several years previously. But it had one remaining use for us. A sandbar had formed alongside it and now it provided fun waves to bodysurf that afternoon. The waves were surprisingly powerful and that evening my shoulders ached from the unaccustomed exercise.

As we were putting up our shelters for the night, the wind came up. It was then that I noticed some white water on the nearby point for the first time.

The rain came early that evening and lightning flashed over the sea. Was it my imagination, or could I make out swell along the point? My last thoughts before I fell asleep were that the sound of surf on the beach was getting louder.

By dawn I was walking north towards the point. The last

clouds were drifting away over the forest and the morning was clear and fresh. No birds were about yet and the only sound was that of waves crashing.

Gradually, as I came closer to the point, I started to make out what all surfers look for when we stare out to sea: head high, almond shaped barrels in crystal water. Long right-handers were gliding over the reef, reflecting the coral on their faces.

With nobody there!

I surfed those waves in my mind for I don't know how long. The take-off looked steep and challenging, but make-able. Then the wave walled up nicely for some manoeuvres on the pristine face, before throwing out a tubing section for about ten metres. The end section provided another fun wall for that searing cutback you would execute after exiting the barrel and then the wave faded into deep water.

I immediately started devising ways of surfing those waves. I fantasised about carving a board out of driftwood. Maybe one of the planks from the jetty would be big enough. Even a boogie board made from some camping mats would do. How I longed to ride those waves!

But I knew that it would be impossible to surf there that day.

Some months later I heard that the jetty had been washed away in a storm. Gone forever, not a trace of it was left. I wondered how big the waves had been on that day and how powerful. Would anyone ever find that place again, without anything to mark the spot?

It was then that I decided that I had to go back to Indonesia to look for surf.

By this stage of our voyage everybody was taking turns to be on anchor watch. We stood watch from eleven o'clock in the evenings till three, when the next person would take over until seven in the morning. The main concern at night was that the anchor could drag and that we would drift onto a reef. It was difficult to find good anchorages in the archipelago, especially since nobody knew the area. So, whoever was on anchor watch would have to monitor any movement of the ship during the night. If it looked like the anchor was being dragged, or if the wind changed and the ship swung too close to a reef, everybody would have to be shaken out of their bunks to pull up the anchor and then the ship would be re-positioned.

We kept an eye on the sonar that measured the depth of the water and the GPS on board made it easy to see how the ship's position changed. We kept a log of our position, the wind direction and so forth during the course of the night, but generally there was a lot of time to kill out on the deck. Anchor watches could get long and drawn out, especially if your sleep had been interrupted to lift the anchor during the previous night. Usually I kept a cup of hot chocolate in my hands for company in the darkness. On land I'm a coffee addict, but at sea I became instantly nauseous if I came near the stuff and for three months I abstained.

In the larder there was a supply of chocolate-covered wafer biscuits named Beng-Bengs, and these were rationed out carefully as morale boosters or at special occasions. To make the supply last, Charmaine hid them away in various places, but there was always plenty of time to search during long anchor watches. The dead of night became a kind of nautical Easter egg hunt for me. I still remember the feeling of sitting on deck, chewing a Beng-Beng and watching the clouds move across the moon. Thinking back on it now, I realise how special those quiet nights had been. The air was always warm and if one was interested, there was always something to look at, even if it was only the reflections of the stars in the water. Sometimes a flying fish would whiz past and splash back into the sea some distance away. Sounds and smells from nearby land would drift over onto the deck, making me wonder about what was there. When we were anchored close to land we'd occasionally see a bat flitting here and there, hunting bugs. We liked the bats; they made the mosquitoes nervous.

That night at Playgrounds we had another downpour. From my bunk I listened to the rain pounding on the deck and I drifted in and out of sleep until at some stage I became aware of a different sound overhead. Together with the rain, there was the sound of running feet, then shouting. I got up to see what was happening and when I came on deck, it was chaos. Amidst the pouring rain and the wind, everyone was running around, pulling on ropes, hauling the anchor and in the wheelhouse Gavin was starting up the engine. The little motorboat that was used to ferry passengers and equipment to and from the ship, called the tender, was submerged alongside the Explorer. It had been moored next to the ship right where the run-off water from the deck went into the sea and so it had quickly been filled with rainwater and had sunk. At the same time the wind had swung around, blowing us in the direction of a shallow reef. By the time the guy on watch had realised what was going on, we were very close to the reef, approaching it fast. To make matters worse, the submerged tender was acting as a sea anchor, preventing us from manoeuvring effectively. At the helm, Gavin was trying to put some distance between the ship and the shallows, but to no avail. He kept dead quiet, his features rigid, his face drained of all colour, wet with rain and perspiration. The alarm on the depth sounder was beeping away, the decreasing depth flashing on the screen: 8m, 6m, 4m … I peered through the rain into the darkness in the direction that we were drifting, but there was nothing to see, the danger was lying under the water. In my mind I saw the jagged edges of the reef reaching out for the hull of our ship – the huge jaws of an eagerly waiting sea monster. The beeping of the depth sounder now turned into a continuous screech, like a heart monitor on a dying patient. At that moment Gavin revved the engine as high as it would go and with an almighty roar the Island Explorer surged away from the reef, pulling the tender out of the water like a water skier behind a ski-boat. You could probably have heard us cheering all the way to Padang as the ship steered for deeper water. Gerhard stepped back from the side wide-eyed. Everybody stood around dumbfounded; the whole episode had lasted only a few minutes. Slowly we sat down in the rain, talking in low voices, marvelling at our narrow escape. This had been close, far too close. Gavin didn't stop the engine. He just kept going way out to sea, away from danger, away from any reefs!

The next morning we woke up to clear skies and calm, clear water in a different bay. The previous night's happenings felt distant, like a bad dream, until we looked into Gerhard and Gavin's faces and saw the dark rings under their eyes.

During the following days we fell into a pattern of searching for various waves, diving spots and of course, safe anchorages. There were plenty of reefs for snorkelling and spear fishing. We landed on the white beaches and collected shells, driftwood and other treasures. You never know what the ocean will yield. On one island Richard turned up with a foot-long phallic carving in wood, with all the detail intact. We had no idea where it came from or what its purpose had been, but we guessed it was some kind of fertility symbol. It was given pride of place at the ship's helm until Charmaine hurled it overboard one day after Pete made yet another ambiguous reference to it.

At this stage of our voyage, most of us had managed to get to know the others on board fairly well. The one person who stayed separate from the rest, however, was Gavin. He avoided mixing with us. At mealtimes, when everyone congregated on the deck behind the galley, he often took his plate of food to the foredeck and ate in silence. During the evenings he spent a lot of time in his cabin. Because Gavin was the first mate, he had less time in the water than the rest of us, but often when he did have free time, he chose to sit in the bow while others went surfing. Nobody really understood why he seemed so offish and people started to gossip about him.

"Did you notice that he always carries a bottle of water

with him?" André was talking to Es.

"Yes, always a full bottle, but I never see him drink. Strange ..."

"Maybe it's not water, it could be cane or vodka ..."

"No! Do you think he's an alcoholic?"

I was wondering about Gavin's mood. At times he seemed down in the dumps, but he would perk up after going diving or when he had some good waves. It was hard to judge how he was feeling because he was so reluctant to speak to us and I did not want to be nosy.

While some of us kept ourselves busy beach combing, I was learning to climb coconut palms in order to get to the fresh coconuts. These are usually higher up than they appear to be from the ground and it was quite intimidating at first, but once I had committed myself to my first tree with an audience on the beach, I had to get at least one of the huge green nuts. It was difficult to prize loose a coconut with one hand while hanging on for dear life with the other and by the time I had finished, I was covered in ants. These ants were not of the average domestic variety that we find at home. They were each as big as a small housefly. At first they were merely an irritation, but as I was making my way down the tree, it was as if one of them gave a signal and they all started biting me at once. I slid down the tree trunk in record time, but by the time I had reached the ground, my body was on fire. While I sprinted for the water, the rest of the boys kindly opened the coconut for me and drank all the juice. I did a frantic ant-inspired dance in the shallows, trying to get them off me and it took a long time to drown all the buggers. Even in death their pincers remained locked onto my shirt and my body. Over the next few days I picked ants out of my shirt's fabric whenever I had a spare moment, but it was never the same again.

Incidentally, the San (Bushmen) people of Southern Africa are said to have been utilising this trait of certain ants for centuries. Apparently they "stitch up" cuts on their bodies by positioning a captured ant or a termite close enough for a bite in exactly the right spot to keep the opposing sides of the laceration together. Once the pincers are in place, they break off the body of the ant behind its head and they repeat the process until they have a row of ants along the wound edges. All of this is easier said than done though; in my experience an angry ant will bite you everywhere except where you want it too.

On the lee side of a tiny island we discovered a playful, wrapping wave that ran into a little bay. This was yet another break that we never identified formally. Whether it is a recognised surf spot I still don't know, but we didn't care. We just rode the waves there until we couldn't paddle anymore. The swell had to wrap around the island, which cleaned up the wave faces until they were silky smooth. Some of the brutish power of the swell had been filtered out by the time the waves arrived in the bay, making them easy to surf, but still a lot of fun. I managed to string together a series of manoeuvres on each wave and that gave me confidence in the water. I could feel a difference in my mood after each successful surf session and this boosted my self-esteem no end.

The person who appreciated this spot the most, however, was Melissa. Because she had only been surfing for a year or two, she found it impossible to venture close to most spots. Derek had bought her a beautiful minimal. (This is a cross between a Malibu board, which is nine feet long or more and a short board, which would be around six feet long.) The advantage of this board is that it has more volume, which is good for stability, but the drawback is lack of speed and manoeuvrability. Indonesian waves demand two things from a surfboard: speed and the ability to weave in the tube. So, more often than not, Melissa sat on deck, mind-surfing the perfect waves, while her surfboard with its pretty floral design and bright colours stood on the board rack in the bow of the Explorer. She never really complained about her situation though. It was enough for her that Derek was having a ball and that he shared his stoke with her. This is as good a measure of true love as any that I've seen.

At our little island, Melissa could jump in the water with confidence and glide along the reef with the rest of us, free as a bird. Derek would sometimes take off together with his wife, riding behind her in the pocket while Melissa would be out on the shoulder. This is what surfing is all about, I said to myself while watching them. Sharing. I thought about my many solitary sessions while trying to improve my ability so that I could look good when I surfed with others. Now I realised that I would have learned twice as fast, had I gone surfing with a friend.

I also thought about Anne. She wouldn't have been able to enjoy this place and while I was relieved that she had been spared the tedium that Melissa had to endure so often, it was hard to be separated from her for such a long time. I wondered what she was doing and how she was feeling. Here I was, drifting around the Indian Ocean on a beautiful white ship, while she had to commute to work and slave away in an office day after day. Did she resent this situation? Was she coping by herself?

During our surf sessions in this little bay, Gerhard still always sat deep, aggressively paddling for all the biggest waves. What his surfing lacked in style he made up for with determination and enthusiasm. I think this attitude pretty much summed up Gerhard's approach to life in general, certainly at that time. But it also caused friction aboard the Explorer. Gerhard's constant hassling in the water irritated some guys. There were enough waves for everyone. Why create tension by trying to out-compete everybody else when you'll get a good wave in a minute or two if you just wait your turn?

Gerhard was clearly used to competition and he liked a challenge. During conversations he would often take a contrary view, just to liven up the discussion. Everything was a contest and if nobody wanted to compete with Gerhard, he would find inanimate objects to have a contest with: climbing the mast and daring himself to jump into the water from that dazzling height; seeing whether he could dive down all the way to the sea floor; or sailing his ship straight through a storm. Although Gerhard could sometimes exasperate people, we were all aware that if it were not for his determination, we would all probably still be working at some drab job, only fantasising about what we were now actually doing. He was that driven kind of person you need to see a difficult project through to the end. He was the reason we were here.

But the person who was affected most by Gerhard's personality was Gavin. Our first mate was the exact opposite of Gerhard. Cautious, risk averse and introverted, Gavin kept Gerhard in check at first. But they had spent a lot of time together before the ship was even near water and by the time the rest of us had joined them, their conversations were terse and restricted to the bare essentials. Gavin was a pessimistic kind of person, nihilistic even, whereas Gerhard would find a way around any obstacle through sheer willpower. Gavin would want to wait out a storm before sailing to the next port; Gerhard would meet it head on and show the bastard who's boss. Unchecked, the one's brash actions could cause damage to the ship and endanger its occupants, while the other would cost us valuable time and cause frustration.

Their disagreements turned into arguments, which became increasingly heated. Gavin started spending more and more time below deck and the only person he would really talk to was Ron. Although I found that Gavin would make quiet conversation with me if we were together alone while on anchor watch, he would clam up instantly if someone else joined us. The little that I could glean from our conversations showed that his outlook on life was negative and that he was angry, with lots of passive aggression waiting to spill over one day. He made me feel uncomfortable, but at the same time I felt sorry for him – he seemed so alone and so gloomy.

Now the words of the Australian ship captain in Padang came back to me. His warning, the one that I had ignored at the time, echoed in my head: "The big brawny Pom, he's completely bonkers."

The rainy monsoon season was slowly drawing to a close, so gradually the weather became drier, with less Sumatran black eyes and more surfable days. When one watches a sleekly edited surf movie, it seems as if the Mentawais have endless perfect waves and blue skies day after day. Of course the videos don't show the down time, of which there is a lot. For every day with good conditions, there would often be an off day. Sometimes the weather would change rapidly, giving us a pleasant surprise in the afternoon after a grey, onshore morning; but often we would have several days of bad weather in a row. You don't read about that very often in the magazines or in the holiday brochures. On those days we sometimes spent entire afternoons lying in our bunks with a book, but generally it was more rewarding to find something ashore if you could motivate yourself to get out into the pouring rain. When the rain was bouncing so hard off everything on the beach that it seemed as if we were under water, amphibious creatures seemed to have a great time.

Mud skippers, those fish that walk around on their fins, breathe air and even climb trees, would often be out and about, dashing around on the flats of the mangroves. The ones we encountered were fairly small, no more than eight centimetres long. They had huge, bulging white eyes sticking out of their brown heads, seemingly on the verge of popping out. They hopped around with a look of perpetual astonishment on their faces. Every so often one of them would leap into the air so fast that it seemed as if it had disappeared and then you'd notice it again a metre or two away, doing push-ups, its entire abdomen heaving up and down, the original gym-bunnie. Of course, as with most behaviour of this kind, it's all just to impress members of the opposite sex in order to get a bit of nookie. Makes you think again about those fitness fanatics who can't stay away from the local health club! The fish were quite territorial and I enjoyed watching different individuals jostling and jumping around each other, vying for a particularly appealing patch of mud. But their tree climbing skills were what impressed me most. Who ever heard of a fish that can climb trees? I'm not sure whether this is to escape predators or to find food (they attempted to eat any living thing that came their way), but that's my kind of fish! Sometimes you'd find one on a branch two meters off the ground. Mudskippers manage to breathe outside the water by using their skin for respiration and they always have to stay moist in order to stay alive.

The other creatures we saw a lot of on the beaches were hermit crabs. They scuttled around everywhere we walked in their makeshift carapaces, always looking for a fight. Sometimes the beach would seem to be alive with jostling shells of every possible shape and size. There were skirmishes all over the place.

If you were lucky, you could sometimes spot a monitor lizard that had ventured away from cover to get some sun, but they were shy of humans and they disappeared into the undergrowth before we could ever get close to them.

When you're in the Mentawais, you obviously want to surf the famous spots. At some stage or another you are going to find yourself at the big name breaks and we were drawn towards them like flies to flypaper. The better surfers on board couldn't wait to sample the perfect waves featured in the surf vids they had no doubt been scrutinizing in slow motion for hours on end. Not to surf them would have been like trekking all the way up to base camp at Everest and then not attempting the summit. But paddling into a double overhead wave at some of the surf spots can be as dangerous as attempting to conquer a serious mountain peak. I don't know of any surfing related deaths in these parts, but the reefs have certainly maimed many.

Gerhard, Jonno and Gavin had been studying the charts, eyeing out Lance's Right – also known as Hollow Trees or HT's – and murmuring amongst themselves. When a new swell appeared one morning, they pointed the bowsprit of the Explorer at the southern tip of Sipura Island and went full steam ahead. It was late morning when we arrived and there were two other boats already anchored at the legendary right-hander. We inched the Explorer as close to the waves as possible and watched the surfers. Most of them were cautiously feeling their way around the line-up, not taking any chances. I could see that they all knew what they were doing. Solid six-foot waves were steamrollering over the reef. When the swell is small, HT's can be fun and even playful, offering some of the best tubes you'll be likely to score anywhere in the world. But when the size increases over six feet, the wave metamorphoses from a feisty playmate to a school bully with psychopathic tendencies. On that day, this was no place for kooks. Water sucked off the reef at an alarming rate, reared up into a menacing lip and slammed down on the reef with a ferocity that is hard to describe. Imagine sledgehammers pounding a brick wall or pneumatic drills pulverising concrete.

If you surf HT's on a big day, you have to be focused and determined. One moment you're paddling for the wave, the next you're stuck in the face of a monster that is trying to hurl you into the coral. The drop is hideously steep and if you're not quick on the take-off, you end up either in a vertical nose-dive or worse, being sucked all the way up with the lip and then getting pitched forward like a banana peel. And it happens to the pros too.

At HT's there was always a crowd, so you couldn't wuss out and take off on the shoulder of the wave. You had to sit right in the critical part of the take-off zone and go deep, otherwise someone else would get the wave. And of course, we all knew what was waiting for us under the surface. We had very little protective gear to shield us from injury. Helmets were of course available and most of the guys on board had one, but we used them relatively infrequently. I think it was a macho, "I'm not scared," kind of thing. To wear a helmet was to admit that you were crapping yourself, which, naturally, all of us were doing a lot of the time. If I were there again now, I would wear my helmet a lot more, even though I'm much more confident in the water now.

To protect your body, the obvious solution would be to wear a wetsuit, but the water was simply too warm to make wearing one practical. I tried surfing with a shorty once, but I became so hot and drained in the suit that I had to take it off after a few minutes. A neoprene vest would have been the right thing to wear, but I hadn't brought one along. I had to make do with my rash vest, which kept the sun off, but gave no protection from abrasions and gouges on the reef.

If you have the motivation and some skill, you can have the ride of your life at HT's and, of course, that was what we were all here for. But I was sitting on the deck of our ship, contemplating the shallow slab of reef in front of the breaking wave, ominously named the surgeon's table. This is where you land up if you straighten out in front of the white water or when you wipe out badly. The water there is knee deep and as the name suggests, the coral is razor sharp. I knew that I had a good chance of visiting the surgeon myself and I eyed my already raw shins with apprehension. I was feeling scared and lonely. I felt that for me those waves could be lethal and that even if I was very careful, there was a good chance of me getting seriously hurt out there. I did not want to paddle into those monsters, but I knew that if I didn't use my chance to ride one of the best waves in the world, I would never forgive myself. I would always be thinking back about the day that I wimped out. So I jumped over the side of the ship and paddled over to the break slowly while trying to think happy, positive thoughts and ignoring the hysterical voice in my head screaming at me to get away from there.

After watching the drama for a while, I edged closer to the impact zone. Eventually I stroked into a relatively weak wave. To my surprise I not only survived the ride, I actually managed to fly over the back of the wave at the end with a semblance of control. I realized that it wasn't that bad after all and I caught a few more of the smaller waves. Surfing HT's is all about getting barrelled, but during my first sessions there the tubes either closed out on me or they were too fast. I had to be content with watching other people getting shacked, kicking out with stoke written all over their faces. Still, I was happy to be there and to be riding waves, even if I wasn't scoring tubes. I wasn't doing too badly. The consensus on board was to stay at HT's while the swell lasted. On some days we surfed the break up to three times and very gradually I started to adjust to the conditions. My confidence improved.

Between sessions we went ashore to the little village of Katiet, where the locals had a tiny shop. There weren't too many goods that we could use, but the people were friendly and it was fun to play with the kids on the beach. A few of them were learning to surf in the shore-break on broken boards that had been left behind by travellers. They had just started to venture into deeper water, surfing a mushy wave in the little bay where they lived, but at that stage hardly any of the villagers were riding the waves on the point that had made their island world famous in surfing circles. I have no doubt that there must be a hardcore group of locals ruling the waves there by now.

Although there was no surf camp in Katiet at the time, quite a few of the local families were accommodating surfers who had caught a ferry to Sipura and who were basing themselves on land.

One of my more embarrassing experiences with the locals occurred one morning early in Katiet. I had woken up hoping for a pre-dawn paddle-out in order to escape the crowd at HT's, but when I paddled over to the break, the waves were messy and an onshore wind came up. Conditions were not good for surfing, so I decided to paddle to shore for a walk. Several older men were squatting high up on the beach, just outside the tree line, contemplating the sea serenely and puffing on the first cigarette of the day. I greeted them in Indonesian as I walked past, but they ignored me, fixing their eyes on the horizon and looking uneasy. I tried saying hello to some of the men further down the beach, with the same awkward result. I was puzzled, because they had all been so friendly and talkative the previous day, but I thought that maybe this was a religious exercise or some form of morning meditation and I left them alone. Only later did I realise that they were all busy with their morning toilet session! A few minutes later the tide came in and washed away any evidence of their presence. I wondered what they did at spring low tide though.

After several surf sessions at Hollow Trees, my confidence had increased to the point where the wave now seemed to be hitting the coral less hard, maybe not quite with the force of a pneumatic drill any more. I started working my way into the line-up to where the serious guys were taking off and one day I found myself sitting near a young pro, who started coaching me into a few waves. Parko was unknown outside Australia at the time, but now he is famous, one of the top surfers in the world. This is probably the closest I will ever come to interacting with surfing royalty. Although I can also claim that more recently Mick Fanning and I paddled for the same wave at Uluwatu and that I eventually got it. (He probably pulled out because it looked too weak. Of course I told everybody that it was out of respect for my red-hot surfing.)

The crowd was relatively thin at HT's that day, the waves were as fun and playful as the place gets and consequently the vibe was fairly mellow. After catching a few smaller ones, a clean looking wall started building on the reef and my new coach called me onto it, but as I paddled into the wave, the thing mutated into a suck-out and it tumbled me around under water. I felt like a bug in a blender. When I came up I was unharmed, but shaken. To compose myself, I decided to take a break and I paddled wide, away from the breaking waves, thinking my own thoughts.

Suddenly everyone was shouting. Three or four waves that were way bigger than anything we had seen all morning were bearing down on us, making everybody scramble to get out of the way of the approaching breakers. It was a freak set and it caught us all by surprise. Because I had been paddling wide, I was the only surfer in position to catch one of the big set waves and the guys were hooting and shouting at me to go. I had no choice ...

At HT's the really good surfers hardly have to paddle to catch a wave. By positioning themselves correctly, they can just push their boards down the wave face and get to their feet. But I had to work hard to catch the wave that was now starting to tower over me. I dug my hands deeply into the water, kept my head down and paddled for all I was worth. At the critical moment I launched myself over the ledge with my heart in my mouth. Somehow I managed to claw my toenails into the wax on my surfboard, staying upright through the vertical drop and then, digging my heels in at the base of the wave, I turned off the bottom in front of this relentless, merciless surge of energy. My eyes were on the dark blue wall ahead of me and I could see it starting to fold over already, blocking out the sun. I could feel myself being drawn up the face of the wave and then suddenly I was inside the biggest barrel of my life, too scared to breathe. I was completely overwhelmed by the sound in there, like the roar of an out of control truck skidding around a bend on a gravel road. In front of me the bright opening of the tube was getting smaller as I was being drawn further back into the maw of the growling monster. Try as I might, I just could not catch up to the light. For a split second I remained poised on my board, standing still in the middle of the swirling chaos and then the next instant I was under water. The sea shook me around as if it had been harbouring a very personal grudge against me for many years and that now finally it got its chance for revenge. A surge slammed me onto the bottom, but I managed to absorb the impact with my feet and up I went again, then suddenly down once more. This time I bumped off the reef on my backside, tearing my board shorts and leaving some skin behind. I think I did two more cycles before I was released. In the aftermath of the wave I floated in the foam, checking whether everything on my body still worked and looking for blood in the water. Miraculously, I was fairly unscathed and so was my surfboard. Little by little, a sense of euphoria crept over me. It wasn't the stoke that follows a great ride, but the realisation that I had survived a proper thumping at this dangerous spot filled me with a sense of achievement and pride. I had managed to pull into the biggest tube of my life and although you could hardly say that I rode the thing, I felt that I had handled the situation well. I made my way back to the ship slowly with a smile on my face. I felt that I would be ok in the heavy surf of the Mentawais.

By this time we had been in the islands for three weeks, so some of the guests on board had to go home and the Island Explorer was due to head back to Padang. I was looking forward to telling Anne about everything we had been doing and seeing. I was already composing letters in my mind, giving (slightly modified) descriptions of the waves and how well I was surfing them. It was around this time that Indie the cockatoo decided to leave Francois for another bird. The ship was anchored at Thunders and we were taking turns to surf. Indie was roaming around on the deck between a few of us who were watching the others in the water. Some lukewarm Bintangs were going down smoothly after our session and we were all in a very relaxed mood. The waves had been fun, the sun was baking down and all of us had aching muscles from paddling back just one more time for that last ride. Some of us were dozing off when there was a shout. Indie was flying away from the ship towards the island. It was a fairly long way to go, and towards the end of her escape she started dipping dangerously close to the water – but Indie made it to shore! She rested briefly on the sand and then flew up into a tree, where another bird was visible between the branches.

Chapter 3
Beyond the Equator

"I couldn't see much; I felt my way along the face of the wave, just taking in the near weightlessness and the smoothness of the water. The lip curled over me and for a second or two I was crouched in the tube, listening to the rush of the sea around me in the darkness. The next moment I was under water as the wave closed out, my ride over – but I surfaced with a smile. I paddled back to the ship soon after this wave. This was how I wanted to remember Nias."

Back in Padang, we had a few days to spend on land while the stores of the ship were being replenished and work was carried out on the engine. Before we went ashore, however, Gerhard convened a meeting. What he told us was not good news. In fact, it felt as if he had dropped a bomb amongst us.

He did not think that the ship was suitable for an Indian Ocean crossing. There had been engine problems and we never made much headway when using only the sails. It would be safer to explore the Mentawais and Sumatra, with the possibility of going up to Malaysia, Thailand and perhaps the Andaman Islands.

The news was devastating. My disappointment was so intense that I just did not know what to think. The grand adventure I had imagined was gone. I love surfing, but I love travelling and exploration more. The combination of the two is perfect, but if I had to choose, discovering wild places and surfing mediocre waves would have been preferable to staying in one place and getting perfect waves every day. My motivation for coming to these islands was to go where very few people ever go. I had thought that this ship was my chance for true adventure. After all, it was named the Explorer! These days one sees so many accounts of so-called extreme expeditions in coffee table books or on television, where minor celebrity presenters report from untamed looking places, but they still get to bring along their make-up artists, security guards and a whole posse of guides to make sure they stay safe. I wanted the real thing and I felt absolutely gutted that my fantasy of macho exploration had been extinguished so suddenly. I was so depressed that I let the others talk me into checking into the Bumi Minang hotel with them. We spent a gloomy evening talking things over and went to bed early.

When I was about sixteen I tore a Mainstay ad out of one of my mother's Cosmopolitans and pasted it to my bedroom wall. I had no idea what cane spirit tasted like and I wasn't especially interested either. What compelled me to have that picture right in front of my desk where I did my homework (apart from the article about finding the g-spot on the reverse side) was that it was a double page spread of two young tanned guys pushing a little row-boat through a breaking wave on a pristine beach into the deepest blue water imaginable. The slogan said, "Escape with Mainstay". It didn't bother me that the two castaways had shaved legs, appeared to be wearing make-up on closer inspection, or that their hair was perfectly styled in the latest eighties fashion. I didn't care about the designer shorts and spotlessly clean white shirts they had on for their escape from their tropical isle. Or even that their only provisions for their no-doubt long and arduous journey was a bottle of Mainstay, sticking out of a pocket at a jaunty angle, soon to be washed overboard by that wave they were attempting to crest.

The captivating thing for me was the fantasy of escaping exams, imbecilic teachers – "Rugby, blah, blah, rugby, rugby … " – idiots on the playground, nerds for friends and the constant gnawing pain of living with a mother with cancer. I knew that I had to stick it out for what felt like an eternity, but that one day, when school and university were over, I would go to that beach on my wall and live that fantasy.

At any cost.

In the meantime, I worked hard at school, played ball sports to fit in and longed for December holidays by the sea, where a single wave would wash away a whole year's frustration and sorrow. We body surfed the gentle breakers in the bay where we own a beach cottage, ran down steep dunes and snorkeled in the murky sea. My father would take me on fishing outings along the rocky coast, where the fish had been plentiful when he was young; by this time, sadly, it had been fished out. On these excursions I pretended that we were on a survival mission somewhere remote and that our lives depended on catching food. My father would sit on the rocks, meditating on the ocean, with his fishing rod idle. "If you sit this far out just staring at the water, people think you are suicidal or crazy and come to rescue you, but if you have a rod they leave you alone," he would say.

When I think back on it now, my Mainstay poster explains why I always wanted to push on further than the others when we were at sea. My shipmates were baffled by my willingness to forever take more punishment on the stormy ocean, even though I was the most seasick-prone person on the ship. I could not tell them why I wanted to press on, why I always wanted to see what was over the horizon. That urge had been developed over many years.

The next morning Ron, Sean and I decided to get rid of our frustration by heading for the hills. I still wanted to climb Bukittinggi's volcano and the trip inland was a welcome diversion. We caught a bus into the highlands and booked in at the Clean Achievement Losmen again. It's strange how the atmosphere in the touristy part of a town can change within a matter of weeks. The group of people that I had come to know when I was there just a few weeks before had moved on and all the faces in the tearoom were different. It was as if I was in another town, but that's the nature of travelling.

The one luxury in Bukittinggi for us Westerners was cheese. Very little dairy is consumed in South East Asia and people here find the notion of eating fermented cow's milk disgusting. The only places where dairy products are available are some of the restaurants that are frequented by tourists. I hadn't had any cheese since I left home almost two months before and I was craving some comfort food. We tucked into pizza and pasta and slurped up every last morsel.

Of course, the new developments on the ship were still on our minds. It was certainly still going to be an adventure to sail between the local islands and to explore the surf. There had to be so many unexplored reefs, points and beaches to be surfed that we could be kept very busy just by searching the Mentawais. Not making long open water crossings would give us much more time for surfing and diving instead of sitting on deck for days on end, waiting to arrive at the next destination. So, although things were turning out very differently from the original plan, the new plan still sounded good – and besides, there was no alternative. I accepted the situation and decided to enjoy the ride, wherever it went.

The next morning we headed to the slopes of Mount Marapi again. En route we stopped at a roadside stall to get some food for the climb. Breakfast in Indonesia has always been an adventure for me. Cereal, porridge or bacon and eggs aren't options here. We looked at the dried fish, rice and various curries and decided to try some deep fried balls of dough, which looked somewhat like doughnuts. We got enough for the midday meal at the summit too.

Conventional wisdom says that breakfast is the most important meal of the day. Many people might find breakfast essential, but usually I just can't stomach food first thing in the morning. I always go for a surf, a run or half a morning's work before I feel ready for food. However, on this occasion I had a mountain to climb and I didn't want Ron and Sean to eat all the food before I got a chance, so I stuffed my cheeks with the doughy balls. But I needn't have worried about losing out on the food. After a bite or two, all of our mouths were on fire. These things were seriously hot! Ron was red in the face and Sean was swigging away at his water bottle as if he was already halfway up the volcano. But we needed the sustenance, so we swallowed the fireballs with lots of sweet tea and tried not to think about lunch!

After my previous attempt at climbing the volcano, I decided not to use a guide this time. I still remembered the way up past the farmlands and we were told that once you were on the main path up the slopes, it would be easy to find the way to the top. The weather was much better on this attempt, with only the occasional downpour. Marapi wouldn't be much of a challenge if you are an experienced mountaineer, but it still takes a day of slogging to climb it; it is 2891 metres high.

Whenever I do long ascents, I find the best technique is to just keep going, no matter how slowly. The trick is to keep putting one foot in front of the other without stopping and before long you leave the mundane world behind you. Once the endorphins start kicking in, the irritations of day-to-day life fade and you can start appreciating the small things. You can literally look down on the rest of humanity and laugh at their frantic rushing around after money and power. Back home in Cape Town we are lucky enough to have Table Mountain right in the middle of the city. From the slopes I have often watched the frenetic activity below and imagined the stressed businessmen rushing around, trying to earn enough money to pay for the huge mansions they live in on the other side of the mountain. Why do so many people create problems for themselves in order to accumulate wealth? I have never understood why someone would choose to work him or herself to death, just so they can buy a fancy car or exclusive clothes to impress others. Does arriving at work in an expensive status symbol really make you any happier than if you had done the commute in an average car? All it means is that you have to spend more time to earn the money for the loan, the insurance, the bond. I'd rather be looking at the chameleons or chasing the butterflies and then go home in my boring old car. Sure, I also work to earn money and when I do work, I work hard. I think that is good. But chasing money for its own sake does not make sense to me.

We arrived at the rim of the crater with aching legs and steam rising from our soaked shirts. There is something special about volcanoes that other mountains don't have. A non-volcanic peak might be challenging to climb and there might be a wonderful view from the top, but to me it does not have that direct connection to the inside of the earth that a volcano seems to have. The smoking crater and the possibility of molten lava spewing out of it fire my imagination. Of course, I wouldn't easily climb a volcano that's on the brink of erupting, but it's great to think that I'm on the slopes of a slumbering giant that is just waiting for its day. Just imagine that the volcano does blow its top like Krakatoa. There couldn't be a more spectacular way to end your existence here on earth than by being launched into eternity by that kind of power! It reminds me a little of the writer Hunter S. Thompson, who had his remains fired out of a canon at his funeral. That was a bit late, though; he was already dead.

The deep pit below us was filled with bare rock and smoke rose from passages deep down. The black sand on the inside formed a stark contrast with the green rainforest on the outer slopes. On the other side far below us, the rice paddies were laid out in geometric patterns and further away still lay Bukittinggi. Everything was green and lush with vegetation. It always looks so peaceful when you're high above it all. We took off our boots and nursed our blistered feet. After going barefoot for the previous month, my feet weren't used to shoes anymore.

Lunch was a fiery affair, appropriate for climbing a volcano. We gulped down the curry balls and started the descent back to base, staying out of farting range from the guy in front of us.

Back in Padang it was muggy and the streets were roaring with cars, scooters and motorbikes. People were still driving like lunatics, and yet again we were surprised not to see any accidents.

I got up early the next morning and walked around the city by myself. Now and then you could still hear the call of the muezzin in parts of the city, with the odd cockerel crowing from within a backyard here and there. I suppose you can call me a morning person. Early in the day I feel energized, positive and adventurous. There is a special atmosphere in the relative quietness of the morning. The humidity and traffic aren't as intense as later in the day and the light is subtle and soft. The people out on the pavements who are sweeping, hanging out washing and beating dust out of mats, seem at peace with the world. The smell of clove cigarettes permeates everything, but it is so ubiquitous that after a while you don't notice it. Then you turn into an empty street and suddenly something isn't there: that sweet, spicy smell is gone and you miss it. (Incidentally, clove cigarettes were invented in the 1880's by a guy called Haji Jamahiri, who lived in Java. In those days people still believed that smoking was good for your health. Haji incorporated cloves in the cigarettes so that he could deliver even more goodness to his lungs. He thought the clove extract helped to alleviate chest pain. The clove cigarettes came to be known as kreteks after the crackling sound that the lighted cigarette made. Unfortunately, Haji died before he could make any money out of his invention. I wonder about the cause of his death, emphysema perhaps?)

After wandering around with my camera for an hour or so, some warungs started to open. It was breakfast time once more and I was still sticking to my principle of trying to experience the local scene as realistically as possible. Across the street was a little restaurant filled with old Indonesian men. This was a no frills establishment catering for the locals and there was no English on the menus. The recently opened McDonalds and KFC joints were popular with many visiting surfers, but, of course, I avoided them. Why even bother to leave home if you're only going to eat American fast food, sleep in rooms decorated with Western posters and not try to mix with the locals? So I walked into the warung with my phrasebook handy and greeted the owner / waiter in Bahasa Indonesia. Although greeting people in their own language (or, in this case, a language that is at least local to Indonesia) is great for breaking the ice and creating goodwill, the trouble is, of course, that people then assume that you can actually speak the language. The owner returned my greeting enthusiastically and then carried on talking, no doubt enquiring about my stay in Padang, my health, my family and so forth. All I could do was to look back at him blankly and shrug my shoulders apologetically. I sat down at a plastic table, grabbed a menu and stared at it for a while. And then I stared at it some more. It was impossible to make any sense of it at all. At one stage I wondered whether I was holding the thing the right way up! There were some basic Indonesian phrases that I knew and I could ask for the prices of items in a shop, but deciphering a local menu not meant for tourists was not one of my strengths. How I wished for one of those Chinese menus with pictures of the dishes! All the patrons in the warung watched me with great interest, but it was clear that none of them spoke a word of English. The owner waited expectantly. To buy time, I tried another Indonesian phrase that by that time I knew well and used often – "I don't speak Indonesian very well". My audience found this most amusing and had a good laugh. With a sheepish grin, I hid behind my menu and tried to think of something to order.

I decided that a boiled egg would be a fairly safe and easy option to explain. I proceeded to act out putting a pot of water on a stove and boiling it, with an egg inside. My audience loved the part where I imitated the chicken laying an egg and they asked for an encore. After much waving of arms and many puzzled facial expressions from the warung owner and all the curious customers, we came to an understanding. I also ordered a cup of tea because that was something I can do with confidence. While I was waiting for my food, I kept myself busy by paging through my phrasebook. As is often the case, some of the other customers came to sit with me and started reading the phrases in the book. They found it hilarious! Soon everyone was taking a turn to read a sentence out loud, to uproarious laughter and applause. I still don't know whether it was the novelty of reading a foreigner's book or the actual meaning of the phrases that was so funny. It did make me wonder about what I was really saying to people when I used the book!

Quite soon, my food arrived. I waited to see what the kitchen had produced with some trepidation and the result was rather interesting. With a flourish my host put down a cup of tea with a raw egg floating inside it. I was a little taken aback, to say the least. But still, it could have been curry balls, or worse, and I didn't want to disappoint my host. So I stirred my egg into the tea and had a taste. It wasn't bad at all. Although I have never thought of making this kind of breakfast for myself since then, it is actually quite a practical, nutritious and time saving meal. It is something my father, who detests cooking, would like. Later on I noticed that it was quite common in Sumatra to have a raw egg in coffee instead of adding milk. I finished my tea and left the warung, to the disappointment of the regulars. That evening they would have a story to tell the wife!

I popped into an internet café to send Anne a last e-mail before we went to the harbour. This would be my last communication with her for a while. Where we were headed, there would be no connection to the world beyond the horizon. Although her e-mails to me were always upbeat, I wondered how she was coping with the loneliness at home.

After getting a few essentials for the voyage, we headed

back to the Island Explorer. Now we were going to explore the least known parts of the Mentawais and then go further north. We were eager for waves and I was hoping that I could improve my surfing to the point where I wouldn't be terrified of waves of consequence.

"What do you guys think of Gavin?" I wanted to know from Sean and Ron. "He can be very morose at times."

Sean had his doubts – "Looks like he's been in the tropics for too long; the heat is getting to him. You can't blame him either. Growing up in England, never seeing the sun and then getting an overdose of it here. It's fried his brain."

"He's not that bad, man," Ron came to the defence of his friend. "He just doesn't get on with Gerhard. You South Africans have a different way of doing things. Sometimes he misunderstands people. He's socially isolated."

"Do you think his judgement is still good?" I pressed the point.

"Yes, I think his judgement is still sound. He's just stressed out."

"As long as he doesn't go completely cuckoo on us," Sean said. "I wouldn't want him to go ape with one of those wrenches he uses in the hold. He's a big guy. Just imagine that we have to lock him in his cabin or something until we get to the next port. Do you doctors carry tranquilisers with you for an emergency?"

"Not that kind. Maybe we can bum a spliff off someone for him ... But seriously, he is the only guy who has real experience of sailing in difficult conditions. Gerhard has sailed in the Med and around Cape Town, but it's obvious that he doesn't have Gavin's experience. And Gavin knows that engine like it's his own mother. Who else will fix it?"

"Yup, we need him."

Sean dug around in his backpack and produced an old, crumpled copy of Surfer magazine – "Check this out." He opened it up at an article written by one Greg Becker about the art of working your way around the world on other people's yachts. According to the article, it's good to have a sought after skill, such as a knowledge of sailing, being a good cook or being a doctor, for instance. There were lots of other tips on how to choose the best passages to good surfing areas. But Sean's grubby finger pointed at these two sentences: "The best trait you can take to a yacht, however, is a good personality. Most sailors would rather sail across an ocean with Forrest Gump than with Hannibal Lecter, no matter how well educated and competent Mr. Lecter might be."

We looked at each other without saying anything.

A pleasant surprise on board for me was that now there was more space after some guests had left and because I was the most seasick prone person on board, I was upgraded to a better cabin. I had it to myself and I immediately made myself comfortable there.

Once we were back on board, we discussed our itinerary. Sean, Derek, Melissa, André, Francois and I wanted to explore as far as possible, but the others were content to stay in the Mentawais. Johnno summed up their feelings: "Fark mate, why would ya go puking yer guts out on the open sea when ya can do it right here where we have waves?" Life was simple for him. When you had money, you surfed until the scratch ran out. When you were skint, you worked until there was enough saved up for the next surf trip. Nothing else came into the equation. Motoring away from waves is one of the cardinal sins of surfing and this went completely against Johnno's grain. Everyone knows from bitter experience that you don't leave good waves to check a distant spot in the hope that the waves would be better there, because they might not be. By the time you've come all the way back to the place you had left, the tide could have changed for the worse or an onshore wind could have come up, ruining your session. When there are waves, you surf, because tomorrow there might not be any. To sail away from some of the best surf on the entire planet for several weeks was utter blasphemy, according to Johnno's Bible.

Gavin was also quite strongly opposed to going far north. The engines could not take too much strain. And "What about our water supply?" he wanted to know. Everybody looked at him curiously.

"For God's sake man – we're in the tropics. It pours down every second day!" was Gerhard's reply.

Gavin fiddled with his water bottle, taking the cap off and putting it back on again. "You've never been without water for long, have you mate? Let's hope you don't find out what it feels like ..."

Fortunately for me, more of us were in favour of going north and so the decision was made.

But our first priority was to get some good, un-crowded waves. We still hadn't had any surf at Macaronis, so we headed out in that direction. When we arrived, we found a weak swell, not big enough to make the spot come to life. Once again Macas was giving us the nautical equivalent of the middle finger.

We spotted a few surfers on the beach, camping under the trees. They looked pretty rough: through our binoculars we could see the sunburn and mosquito bites on their shirtless bodies. Intrepid surfers who did not want to go on a charter boat often hired a fisherman to drop them off on an island and to pick them up again a week or two later. I suppose these guys were really hoping that the boat wouldn't sink on its way to come and fetch them again! We had been ashore at Macaronis before, just long enough to pick a coconut or two and to confirm that the mosquitoes there were big, plentiful and hungry. The feral surfers were camped close to the island's swamp, the perfect breeding ground for these bloodsuckers.

In addition to the mosquitoes, there would be boredom to contend with for those who choose to camp on a deserted island. There isn't much to do in paradise when the weather and waves don't play along. If you can't surf or go snorkelling, what do you do? Beach combing or exploring the interior of the island lose their appeal after a few hours. Having no facilities means you must be well equipped for camping and if you forgot the sugar or something, you can't go and buy it at the corner shop. I remember once forgetting the salt on a similar excursion, but I wasn't fazed. After all, the sea is full of salt water. Instead of cooking with fresh water, I just cooked with seawater. After choking down a few spoons-full of extremely salty oatmeal for breakfast, I discovered that the sea is a lot saltier than I had previously believed! But you learn to improvise.

We turned the Explorer around and headed south for Rags and Thunders once more, leaving the feral surfers on shore to read that dog-eared surfmag they brought along for flat days one more time.

The swell was hitting Rags just right and if you were good, you could get some great barrels. If you weren't, you ended up standing waist deep on the reef, being pounded by head high walls of white water. I discovered that the reef at Rags is especially sharp and that just touching the coral can lead to deep cuts. After surviving a set or two on the reef, I managed to launch myself back over the oncoming waves and I made it out into the line-up again. I watched Jonno coming out of a few tubes and Sean snagged a good one as well, but I turned my back on them and headed to the ship to apply some painful wound care to my legs. I had a few gashes in one calf that were bleeding rather enthusiastically.

Making sure that reef cuts don't become infected is paramount in the hot, humid conditions of the equator, ideal conditions for bacteria to grow. Some very nasty and persistent bugs live on coral and they can cause terrible sepsis if given the chance to multiply in the tasty flesh of a hapless surfer. This means that whenever you cut yourself on the reef, you have to make sure you exterminate these nasties by pouring some very caustic chemicals into your raw wounds. The abrasive of choice for most surfers is hydrogen peroxide, the stuff other people put on their hair to look cool if they're not naturally blonde enough. It bubbles and fizzes and produces a bloody pink foam that boils out of the wound. You sweat, you swear, you pray and you whimper. To make sure any coral debris in the wound has been removed, you scrub the wound with a toothbrush and then rinse with sterile water. There is always an audience when you give your cuts the peroxide treatment. Your mates laugh long heartless laughs, because they know that you are going to laugh at them when their turn comes. And it will come. They know that too.

Finally, some antibiotic powder is applied and the wound is covered with gauze. You are now free to pass out.

Alas, it wasn't just my leg that had been injured during my reef dance. Once again, my surfboard had been damaged on the reef, so I took one of my other two boards out of storage in the bow of the ship. Before we had docked at Padang, I had dinged that board during another of my less successful surf sessions at a spot called Bank Vaults, a wave that takes you deep into its dark recesses. The only way to ride it properly is to pull into the tube and then to try to make it onto the shoulder of the wave from way back behind the falling lip. I didn't make it out of any tubes during that session, but I did manage to negotiate my way through some sections of the wave and I was getting the feeling that my surfing was progressing. I was starting to adapt to the fast breaking reef waves. But Vaults claimed a chunk of my board during that session and reminded me that I still had a long way to go.

I had decided to let the tear in the fibreglass of that damaged surfboard dry out while we were ashore and then to fix it on my return. What I found when I got back was that some ants had made a nest inside my surfboard. They had entered through the broken fibreglass and had burrowed tunnels into the foam. Everything in this part of the world seemed hardier than at home, even the ants. I eventually managed to cut out most of the nest, but some ants remained and had to be sealed inside my board. You could faintly make out their bodies through the resin, entombed deeply inside their unusual nest. That surfboard lasted for a few more years after the trip and back home in the cold Cape water the ants were always there to remind me of Indonesia.

It was time to head north, so we started our journey past some of the lesser-known islands. Gradually we saw fewer of the other charter yachts and when we found waves, we generally had them to ourselves.

But Gavin was not happy. "What if we run into trouble now? There will be no other boats to help us. We could die of thirst if we lose engine power far from land."

"This is a sailing ship, remember?" Gerhard was irritated. "Anyway, there are settlements in the most unlikely places on these islands. We're sure to get help if we really look."

"What if there's no wind and we run out of water? These parts aren't known as the Doldrums for nothing." He compressed the sides of his water bottle in his hand, flexing the walls in and out, taking the cap off without drinking.

Gerhard's response was to walk away and to start hoisting sails. Francois was on deck soon, pulling hard on the ropes of the main sail as it slowly spread out in the breeze. The rest of us pitched in as well and before long the sails filled with wind. I would not say that we were absolutely flying – the ship was too awkward and its crew too inexperienced – but we were sailing after a fashion and it felt rather good to be gliding along in such an effortless, noiseless and exhaust-free manner.

Gavin skulked off, muttering dark words and crumpling his water bottle in his fist.

One morning we sailed into a deep bay flanked by high hills, completely covered in green indigenous trees. We could see coral heads under the surface of the crystal clear water in the middle of the bay as we slowly glided over them. Ahead of us there was a small white beach and to complete the fantasy-setting, there were waves peeling endlessly along one side of the bay. There was a catamaran anchored close to the beach, providing a point of focus for a perfect picture. The island itself was uninhabited. Even though we still had a long way to go northwards, we decided there and then to drop anchor and to stay a while.

On the cat there was a family comprised of a teenage son and daughter and their parents. They had sailed from Australia and were exploring the islands in much the same way that we were doing. They said that they had surfed the waves we had been looking at and they had named it the Widow-maker. I looked at the tough, no-nonsense father and his strapping son and decided to skip the session there. I didn't want to turn Anne into a widow before we were even married.

The water in the centre of the bay was deep enough not to be disturbed by wave action and conditions were perfect for free diving. By that time I had been snorkelling almost every day when conditions allowed and my lungs were in good condition. I descended easily through the warm water towards the coral about ten meters below the surface. At that depth the water filters out a lot of colour, reducing the intensity of red, orange and yellow. But this reef was so rich in diversity that it was still beautiful. There were sponges, fronds, fans and countless kinds of hard coral in different colours. Various types of angelfish, butterfly fish, moonies, jumping beans and a domino or two were feeding on the reef. Many of these fish go through changes in colouring and patterning as they grow from juveniles to adults, adding to the diversity of what I saw before me. There were striped individuals, spotted fish and even some with spirals on their flanks. They were splashed with colour, as if a modern painter had designed them. You can see why people would think that nature was made for the gratification of us humans. Why else would these beautiful things be around? But I feel the opposite is more likely: that people probably developed a liking for the aesthetics in nature, having been conditioned through millennia of exposure to it. These fish have been around on earth much longer than humans.

I knew that if I were able to hold my breath for long enough, some bigger fish would appear from around a corner. I just had to wait a while. When your time under water depends on a lung full of air, you can't expend any energy on unnecessary actions. Every move you make uses oxygen and shortens your bottom time. So I pointed my head to the seabed and let gravity take me downwards, gliding along with just a flick of a swim fin now and again. At the bottom I held on to a dead piece of coral and waited to see what would appear.

After a while I looked over my shoulder and spotted a curious face behind me. A rock cod was checking me out, but it disappeared the moment I turned to face it. All I was left with was a swirl of sand from the ocean floor and the image of a spotted red body in my mind. On the periphery of my vision I could see flashes of silver along the edges of the reef. These I knew were predators such as kingfish, trevally and the like. I think they prefer open water, but the reefs, which were well stocked with prey, also attract these hunters. They were fast and sleek, darting in to make a kill and then disappearing again. Unfortunately for them, these were the fish that the spear fishermen on board would seek out later. It's a shame that we have to destroy these beautiful fish in order to eat. Against a skilled diver with a spear gun they stand no chance.

I swam back to the ship after an hour or so of drifting around the reef. It was lunchtime and Charmaine had freshly baked bread on the table. This was something that I really enjoyed. Every morning it was someone else's turn to bake bread. Francois taught me the recipe.

"It's very easy bru, anyone can do it. You take a bag of flour and mix it with a bowl full of water, some yeast and a pinch of salt. Keep going till the dough is nice and uniform, not too sticky. Knead it well, then you cover it and leave it in the sun for half an hour. Then you knead it down again. You'll see that it cleans all that gunge out from underneath your fingernails beautifully. You know, the stuff you can't get out with a nail file. It's great for getting rid of that black grease and oil from working on the engine."

"Eugh!"

"Bru, everyone has a secret ingredient when it comes to good recipes. I just told you mine for free! And people love my bread. Just pop it in the oven for an hour and lunch is ready."

He was right. My nails were never cleaner than on my baking day and my bread was popular too!

At lunch the guys who took on the Widow-maker reported that actually it wasn't that intimidating at all, just some clean running walls on which to cut loose. The place didn't really barrel; it was a mellow wave for a change. André and I paddled out for an afternoon session and it was great to be able just to relax in the surf for a change. I didn't have to worry about getting caught inside by a big set or of being driven into the reef by another killer wave. Make no mistake, if we fell, we could still encounter the reef with the usual consequences, but at least the wave wasn't actively trying to kill us. André and I could try to push our turns a little further, take off later and laugh at each other. He was a better surfer than me, but not by that much, so it was good to share waves with him. In real life he was a chartered accountant; he was not always keen on doing the mundane jobs on board the ship. As he put it, he was good at delegating tasks. Often we'd find ourselves scrubbing the deck or whatever, with André giving friendly, helpful advice by our side, working on nothing except maybe his tan. But he was a witty and fun bloke to have around.

We made it back on board just in time to see what was for supper. Richard, Gavin and Gerhard were all keen on spear fishing and they had done well for us that afternoon. Richard posed proudly with a large Kingfish, with other, more brightly coloured fish lying at his feet. Derek was sharpening a knife, getting ready to prepare a feast for the evening. He was an enthusiastic cook.

I was also admiring the catch, grateful for the food. The thought of a good Indonesian fish curry made my stomach grumble; you can't get fish any fresher than this.

Part of me was feeling sad, however, and I had to ask Richard, "Don't you feel bad about shooting the fish when they are swimming around so freely, to destroy these beautiful creatures for our pleasure?"

"We have to eat, haven't we? And there simply isn't enough fruit and vegetables available for us over here. We need to do this in order to survive. What would you do if I didn't go out to hunt?"

"If I have no alternative, I would also shoot fish to survive and I have done so in the past, but I don't enjoy it. I feel so guilty."

"Well, it's not as if we just kill for pleasure. This isn't trophy hunting. I don't go out to bag a fish that I can mount and display on my living room wall. And I'm not one of those guys who pay huge sums of money to go and hunt lions or elephants just to satisfy my lust to kill or to boost my ego. I don't enjoy the blood and gore."

Melissa joined us. "I think modern technology has made hunting easier on the conscience," she said. "The hunter can be almost completely detached from his prey. Just think of telescopes on hunting rifles. You can pick off a buck from so far away that you can't see the expression in its eyes when it dies. Trophy hunting reminds me of a child squashing the life out of ants just for the hell of it. And people call it sport!"

"Aggh, don't be such a bunch of sissies! Do you want us to have a memorial service for each fish we eat? Do you lot apologise to each I&J cutlet you defrost at home?" Gerhard was a little indignant. "Anyway, it's in our blood; it's in our genes. People have been doing this for ages. It is part of our make-up, primal and essential. If primitive man did not hunt, we would never have survived as a species."

"Yes, but not everything that people have done over the millennia is still acceptable," Melissa said. "Just because something used to be common doesn't make it right. Rape and abduction used to be widespread and acceptable – just think of the Vikings. It might even have had good effects, like diversifying the various gene pools; but we don't tolerate this sort of behaviour any more. We have moved on."

Gavin had been listening to the conversation quietly. "Hunting buffalo on foot with a bow and arrow would be good sport," he chuckled. "Hey, if things don't go your way, you die. Fair's fair."

The following morning the surf was flat, so we said goodbye to the yachties and motored further north. An onshore wind came up, ruining our chances of finding waves and making the passage rough. There was little to do on board while we were motoring onwards. Although I wasn't really seasick, the choppy sea made me rather queasy, so reading was not an option. We were steering away from land, heading in a straight line towards our destination for the evening, a small group of islands near a village that Gerhard knew about from a previous trip.

When you are out on the open sea, there is generally a lot of water, sea spray and wetness, with very little to look at or to do when it's not your shift on duty. The days can become long. We were thinking of all the islands we were passing by on our way north. How many world-class waves were we missing? But when the weather is bad, it is better to stay on the move. We could look at these islands again on our return journey and I was still very keen on going as far as we could range. The Andaman Sea sounded exotic and I wanted to experience it.

For distraction, those of us on deck had long, rambling conversations. Ron told me about his experiences as an investment banker in London. He was there during a boom time and there was a lot of work available. If you were good enough, you could bluff your way into a lucrative job. Employers needed to fill positions and there weren't enough applicants. The corporate types were not fussy.

"Did you have any qualifications for the job?" I asked.

"No mate, not a scratch. I started a business degree back home, but I couldn't be arsed to finish it. What they were teaching us was worthless anyway. I would have left there with a certificate, but no real skills. I ditched the course and applied at the University of Real Life. Fixing dings in Polynesia taught me more about economics than the professors ever could. Then I went to London and made some dosh."

Ron got a smart suit, some natty ties and charmed the receptionists so that he could get his "CV" on their bosses' desks. Initially, through a mixture of luck and common sense he achieved a good deal of success, enough to be promoted to a position where he could hire junior staff. Of course, he had no idea what to look for in an assistant, so he chose only the attractive girls who were single and he hoped that they would want to assist him in more ways than just with investments.

"And how did the extracurricular side of the job go?" I wanted to know. He just smiled mysteriously behind his sunglasses and looked out at the white caps on the water.

In the end Ron had to leave the firm he had been working for rather hastily. The investments that he had been looking after weren't doing well anymore and he was fielding increasingly difficult questions from management every day. So he bought a business class plane ticket to France on the company credit card and got out.

Late in the afternoon we spotted land. Gerhard had some information about the area and apparently there was a surfable wave close to a safe anchorage. We dropped anchor near a little settlement with the sun nearing the horizon. There was smoke rising from chimneys in the village as people started to prepare the evening meal. We could smell burning coconut husk and hear children's voices faintly. There was still enough time left for a quick surf before darkness came and a few of us paddled over to a little wave close to where the Island Explorer lay. A light onshore wind was still blowing, but there were some fun rights and it was great to loosen our muscles after the long day at sea. Soon we attracted an audience. A group of about twenty kids and some men sat on a fallen tree at the shoreline and cheered as we rode the waves. Every ride was celebrated enthusiastically and the atmosphere reminded me of the excitement I felt on the arrival of the circus in our town when I was a boy. What a feeling! Even though we could not speak each-other's languages, we had something in common here that allowed us to communicate. They understood the sea and they knew the power of the waves breaking on their shore. From navigating these waters with canoes and small boats daily, they understood what we were doing and they showed their appreciation by applauding our rides. I had read about similar situations in surf magazines before, but it was special to be part of this interaction that happened so spontaneously.

After a while I decided to go left on a few waves, which provided a much shorter ride and ended in shallow water, necessitating a kind of flying exit over the back of the wave. This drew by far the loudest cheers. Clearly, this was a new approach for the audience and although my surfing wasn't anything spectacular, I think they liked the change.

Because we had been sailing all day long, there had been no chance to dive for supper, so we had the usual spaghetti with tomato paste and chilli sauce, followed by a Beng-Beng for desert. We went to bed early and I hoped that my anchor watch would not be too eventful. One never knew what to expect at a new anchorage.

During the night the ship had started to rock back and forth and in the morning we saw that the swell had increased in size. Waves were now breaking on an outside reef and they were much bigger than the previous evening. It was time to wax up my longest board. I tried not to look too nervous as I swallowed down an extra cup of instant noodles for energy. Some of the guys were already paddling towards the reef.

Wave size is always a contentious issue among surfers. First of all there is the issue of whether one judges wave height from the back or from the front. A wave that is three feet high from the back can have a much bigger face, maybe six feet, so you have to make sure you know what system the person you are talking to is using. In addition to the above, calling the height of a wave involves a lot of popular psychology. If you say a wave that you have surfed was six feet high and your buddy who surfed the same session calls it three feet, you obviously look like a wuss for overestimating the conditions. Conversely, your friend now appears very macho, apparently having charged into six-footers as if they were only three feet high. Or, if you are checking the waves from the beach with some other surfers and someone thinks the waves are five feet, you can try to look cool by saying "Nah, it's just three feet." Even better is to describe the scary overhead wave you had just kicked out of to the awed grommets on the shoulder as a nice little three-footer. They now think you have balls of steel.

Early on in my surfing life I went to Bali once after working in Borneo for a month. The surf was good and the atmosphere was brilliant; but I struggled to get enough waves at the busy spots, so I took a ferry over to Nusa Lembongan Island to try to escape the crowds. On my first full day there I got up before dawn and I paddled out across the lagoon in the dark to a spot named Shipwrecks. This place is more serious than the soft beach breaks at Kuta on Bali, but not as intimidating as the more challenging spots in the Mentawais. For me at that stage however, it was pretty heavy and the waves looked huge. There were only three of us out at first, as most guys wait for a boat ride out to the reef. This was perfect for me, because I had more room to manoeuvre into a comfortable take-off spot and I managed to get a few good rides, even ducking under the lip for a fraction of a second on (in my overawed eyes) a solid eight-footer for what I thought was my first tube. As I paddled back out after this exhilarating wave, a grizzled Aussie caught up with me and congratulated me: "Great wave mate, you almost got a little cover-up. Must have been at least three feet on the face!" I was completely devastated and I went in shortly afterwards.

As can be expected, the Americans have taken this kind of bragging to the extreme, especially in Hawaii. Ten feet Hawaiian is closer to twenty feet in actual size.

So, let's just say that on this morning somewhere in the Indian Ocean north of Padang and south of Nias the waves were definitely bigger than overhead. I was waxing my 7'0" board while wishing that I was going to surf over sand rather than shallow coral; that I had a bigger board; that I was more experienced than I was; that everyone would just shut up about how big the waves were, or better still, that I had an excuse not to paddle out.

For me the most intimidating thing about surfing bigger waves is the moment when I see the wave coming towards me and I know I have to turn my back on it and paddle out in front of that huge mound of water in order to catch it. With the crest towering over my body, about to come crashing down with all its weight and power, I feel a coldness inside me. I suppose everyone experiences the same urge to just paddle for the horizon over the back of the wave, to escape it, to get the hell out of its way. But if you want to experience the thrill of becoming part of this immense concentration of energy, to run before it for a few seconds and to feel that incredible acceleration and speed, you have to ignore your fear and go against your instincts.

There is no easy way into a big wave, but the moment I swing around and commit to it, the fear disappears and then only the wave matters. The feeling that follows for the next fleeting moment or two is what keeps all of us coming back for more. It is futile to try to describe it; words are too concrete and rational to convey the experience.

I had a good session that morning. I made most of the take-offs and I didn't hit the reef. And for a few seconds on some of the bigger waves I glimpsed heaven. I felt an intimate affinity with the waves and with nature. With my veins full of adrenaline from the effort and exhilaration, I experienced the bliss that so many religions describe. I could see where epiphanies, revelations and visions came from and I found myself close to that exalted state so often described by charismatic faiths.

Towards the end of the session a yacht sailed into the sheltered area close to where we were surfing. A man with long grey hair and a deep brown tan, dressed only in a pair of trunks, came on deck and dropped the anchor about a hundred meters from the break. He paused and watched as I took off on a wave and for a moment while I was standing there with my fingers brushing the water's surface, our eyes met. Neither of us said or shouted anything. We didn't wave or acknowledge each other; there were no clichéd hand signals or whooping shouts. We just looked into each other's faces across that distance between the yacht and the wave and then there was a flicker of a smile on his face, some recognition. I don't think he was a surfer; he never ventured into the waves while we were there. But, like the islanders the previous evening, he seemed to appreciate what we were doing. We never met, but it felt like we knew each other after that brief encounter. I liked him.

As we sat on deck afterwards with a beer each and reflected on the session, we talked about that almost spiritual aspect of surfing. Many people have drawn parallels between surfing and Buddhism and a whole generation of hippy surfers has explored this relationship. This departure from Western religion and, of course, the drug culture that went along with it had made surfing almost taboo where I grew up.

"Did you know that surfing is now officially registered as a religion in the States?" Sean asked Francois.

"Ja, but I think it's mostly so that certain surfing organisations can get government funding. If you are a religious institution, you are entitled to money over there."

"Would you consider surfing to be a religion though?"

"I think almost any activity can take on religious qualities if your mindset is right. Sometimes surfing feels like a religious experience to me, when I'm surfing some idyllic spot by myself and I'm feeling peaceful and happy."

"But a close final in a competition with the opponents ready to annihilate each other hardly qualifies as a spiritual experience."

"Some church services that I've been to hardly qualify either!"

"I suppose it really depends on your definition of religion and of God."

"Have you ever considered a wave as a metaphor for God? Think about it. A wave is an immense, unstoppable, impersonal force that surges ahead regardless of what is happening around it. When you are in the water, as far as you are concerned, that wave is omnipotent. Nothing influences it; no prayer or sacrifice will change that wave, but if you approach it with the necessary knowledge and respect, you could use it to your advantage. You can tap into an incredible power source."

"Is that your definition of God?"

"Sometimes …"

The conversation was interrupted by the appearance of a typical Indonesian fishing boat in the bay. It came put-putting around the point and dropped anchor not far from us. On board were some white boys who were looking over in our direction in a fairly nervous way. The Indonesian skipper and his deck hand sat in the shade behind the cabin, smoking kreteks, while their passengers waved to us. Soon one of them jumped overboard and paddled over to the Explorer on a surfboard.

Their ambassador, called Todd, stood dripping on the foredeck and he looked rather desperate. "Boy, am I glad to see y'all! We didn't think we'd survive the night. Did y' see the storm out there? Felt like a damn hurricane! Why, we all strapped our biggest surfboards to our ankles and we were hollerin' for help at the heavens, just waitin' to be taken down by a big wave. Even Jeff the agnostic was prayin! We were sure grateful to see y' here when we came into the bay. Such a big ship, betcha didn't even feel the swell."

"Ja well, we were lucky to be in this protected anchorage," Gerhard said. "Where are you from in the States?"

"East coast, all over. I'm from North Carolina. This is our first time in Indonesia. Pretty hectic! The boat captain don't speak any English. He just says 'yes' to everything we ask him. Last night we wanted to know where we were going to shelter.

He just said 'Yes, no worry.' We asked him for life jackets and he said, 'Yes, no worry.' But there ain't no life jackets in that tub. I thought we were all gonners for sure. I don't know how we survived the night. Felt like forever. We were all of us so seasick; we can't stomach food. Not that there is much to eat. All they have aboard is dried fish, chillies an' noodles. Breakfast, lunch and dinner, the same again and again. Can't face it no more!"

"How many of you are there?" Gerhard asked rather nervously. It was obvious where this conversation was going.

"Just the six of us, but there ain't enough room for shelter for us all. We have to take turns to sit in the shade. Too hot inside the cabin and it stinks of gasoline. That boat-captain just sits an' smokes those god-awful clove cigarettes right next to the gas. We're just waiting for it all to explode. And all of us are sunburnt. The sun just roasts you alive out on that deck. Not long now an' we would have used all our bottled water and then we have to depend on the captain's supply. Don't know how clean that is and him an' his deck hand backwash in it all the time when they drink. God knows, they don't look none too healthy."

"Did you get any good surf at least?"

"Surf? Haven't even given it a thought! We're just survivin', man! Fuck surfin'. We just want to get out of this place. I don't care if I never see a surfboard again in my life. Which way 're you-all headed? Goin' back to Padang? We could sure use a lift if y' could fit us on board. We got money. We'll pay ..." His eyes pleaded forlornly with Gerhard, then he looked at each of us in turn.

"Jeez, I'm sorry bru, but we're going north, to Nias. That's in the opposite direction that you want to go in. It's two or three days' sailing from here and we can't turn around now. We can give you some food and water, but we don't have that much for ourselves."

After a while Todd paddled back to their boat and deliberated with his friends. They hung around for a while and a few of them even paddled over to the wave on the inside reef for a surf, but they were listless in the water and after a short while they returned to their vessel. Later on they got ready to leave and came alongside our ship to say goodbye.

We gave them what food we could spare and wished them good luck. At the last minute Charmaine's softer side got the better of her and to the horror of the chocoholics on board, she donated a quarter of our Beng-Bengs. "Just don't give them our water," was all Gavin said. He twirled the cap of his bottle in his fingers and went below.

As the little fishing boat disappeared over the horizon, I thanked my lucky stars that I had not ended up in a similar situation.

Our larder was now very low on fresh produce, so Richard and I decided to paddle over to the island in the kayak in search of a shop of some kind. Richard and Gerhard felt that the best route would be the direct one across the reef that we had surfed at during the previous evening. They identified a keyhole in the reef that we could dart through during a lull in the sets. This was the channel that the lefthander I had surfed the evening before was running into. Thinking of the flying kick-outs that I had been forced to do at the end of my rides, I was hesitant about the proposition of steering a kayak into that little channel. The end section slammed down on the coral and the waves were bigger than the day before. But the general consensus was that this was the best way, so we waited behind the waves for the right moment and with lots of very vocal encouragement from those on deck, we started to paddle briskly through the gap. Everyone who's ever tried to come in to shore over a reef or rocks would know the sinking feeling of looking over your shoulder after committing to that final dash for safety and seeing a dumper bearing down on you from behind. I saw what was coming, but there was nothing to do other than hold on and do the all-too-familiar "landing feet first" routine when we were unceremoniously upended, kayak and all. I came up with my paddle in one hand and the bucket we had taken along for carrying vegetables in the other. Richard was holding on to the kayak and we waded ashore, amid loud cheering, applause and witty comments from those on the mother ship. A quick look around on land revealed a few huts, but no produce of any kind. A lone fisherman who sat mending a net under a tree pointed towards the neighbouring island, so we launched the kayak again and returned to the Explorer, managing to stay afloat this time.

After lunch a group of us of us headed towards the next island in the tender. We moored at a wooden jetty and walked along a tree-lined road into the village. Our reception was enthusiastic and boisterous, although communication was somewhat limited. Throngs of children ran up and down in the street chanting "Hello Mister! Hello Mister!" and the bolder ones managed "Gimme sweets!" That seemed to be the sum total of English spoken on the island and we were grateful that Gerhard and Jonno could speak some Indonesian. Bahasa Indonesia, the official language of Indonesia is of course not these islanders' first language. They have their own native tongue and they learn Bahasa at school. English would not have been of much use to them.

It was fun walking among the milling children who were holding our hands, jumping up and down and enjoying the novelty of meeting exotic visitors. How refreshing not to have the feeling that we were about to be scammed or taken advantage of at any moment, like in so many foreign places.

The main road through the village was paved with white crushed coral and the rest of the tracks were sandy. The buildings were mostly made of wood, with corrugated iron roofs. Set slightly apart from the rest of the dwellings was a small mosque, also with a corrugated iron roof. There were banana, papaya and palm trees everywhere between the houses and most yards had a vegetable garden. An informal shop was selling a few basic commodities and here we managed to buy some vegetables and fruit from the shopkeeper's garden. On a nearby wooden deck some small silver fish were being dried and next to these a boatload of sea cucumbers was also baking in the sun. This type of sea slug, also known to connoisseurs of haute cuisine by the exotic name of beche-de-mer, is prized in the East as an aphrodisiac, a source of protein and for various alleged healing properties. Going by the smell of these slugs, which look suspiciously like dried turds, I'm glad I'm not Chinese. I wonder whether the members of the exclusive gastronomic societies of the world know that the precious beche-de-mer is a slimy slug that crawls around on the sea floor, eating whatever debris might be floating around it and engaging in group-sex whenever enough of them can get together. (It has a relative, the sea hare, which lives a very simple life, using a single orifice for eating, reproduction and excreting functions. Comparatively, the sea cucumber is very sophisticated, with a separate mouth, thus avoiding the obvious hazard of eating its own shit from time to time, not to mention halitosis.)

As far as we could see, fishing and the harvest of sea cucumbers were the only industries here that could be seen as commercial. People ate what they could catch and cultivate and if they needed anything else, they had to buy these things elsewhere by taking the sporadic local ferry to another island in the general vicinity.

To me life seemed idyllic and uncomplicated in this little settlement, with no rushing around and very little stress. It wasn't possible to accumulate great wealth here and there was nothing much to spend your money on anyway. People did not compete with each other for money or possessions. This was the kind of village you dream of escaping to when life in the city gets too much. But of course the trouble is that when things go wrong here, relatively minor problems can turn into a disaster. People had no access to medical care, no insurance and no outside support. In the past I used to fantasize about rolling the dice myself and moving to a remote place such as this village for a year or two. Here I would live the simple life, only surfing, fishing, diving and reading. For a single guy without responsibilities this could have been fun for a while. But I suppose most of us would like social contact with people of our own culture and at least some sort of medical back-up plan, especially when we become older. So we return to our safe, but comparatively boring lives. In order to pay for the security of being taken care of when we become unwell or old, we spend our lives working and paying medical insurance, often doing jobs we come to hate. On the positive side, at least I live in a part of the world that has been geologically stable up to now.

It has been many years now since our brief stop at the tiny village in those remote islands and since then at least three earthquakes and one devastating tsunami have occurred in the area. The Mentawai Islands are a paradise, but they are located right on the brink of the Sunda Trench, where tectonic plates collide with incredible power, causing massive upheavals. When a piece of ocean floor is jerked up or down with the might that moves continents, the effects can be devastating. Submarine earthquakes can produce tsunamis that move at up to a thousand kilometres per hour. In the case of the big tsunami of 2004, the waves weren't moving as fast as that, but because the tsunami was produced so close to land there would have been no warning or time for escape for the people here. There was no barrier between the open ocean and the village and the entire island would have been engulfed by water. I wonder now what had become of the simple homes, the little jetty and all the laughing children when the tidal wave came. The disaster happened about four years after our visit, just a blink of an eye in geological terms. If you look at it from this perspective, we had a narrow escape.

In my mind's eye I can still see the modest mosque standing apart from the other buildings, the earth around it swept clean, its doors open to whoever felt the need to go inside for guidance or support. But I wonder about the God that these villagers believed in and which they worshiped there. Would they still believe that their God exists after the death, destruction and suffering caused by the tsunami? How can anyone believe in a just and loving God who allows atrocities like these to afflict whole communities? I don't know whether there were any survivors from the village to answer these questions.

Somewhere on a remote island in the vicinity of Nias a crazy Belgian opened a bar and strung up a few hammocks to sleep in. Sometimes a few surfers would brave the swarms of malarial mosquitoes and stay in his camp, drink his beer and surf themselves silly on the incredible waves at Asu. This Belgian did not surf or dive or fish. Nobody knows why he ended up on his island in the middle of nowhere. Of course there are the stories about drug smuggling, running from Interpol and more, but we never found out who he really was and why he chose to stay on Asu. I can't remember his name any more. Something like Vincent. He was gregarious and interesting to talk to. He had strong opinions about most things and eventually he always fell out with whomever it was that he was talking to. He wasn't very diplomatic. It must get lonely on this island during the off-season, especially if you piss off the few visitors who do come by. I wonder whether he is still there …

When we arrived at Asu it was most definitely not the off-season for surf. We had followed the swell that had reached us at the little village to the south and now the people on deck were looking at some very big waves exploding along Asu's reef. I was still in my bunk, passed out with seasickness from the rough crossing. And maybe I was also a little reluctant to face this wave. The boys had been talking about it on the way and it sounded nasty. The take-off is way on the outside, with a fast section that has to be negotiated quickly after getting to your feet, otherwise you end up getting shut down by the white water and eating coral. Then there is a long, hollow section, with barrels and room for manoeuvres on the open face. Just when you think you have mastered the wave, you enter the "nuclear zone" and you get blasted straight onto dry reef if you don't kick out in time. Asu is a world-class wave with world-class consequences if you're not careful.

Jonno, Gerhard, Francois and Sean were straight out there, scratching their way into some bombs. The waves were so big that it took ages for them to get to the bottom after take-off. I came on deck and watched with binoculars. Gavin didn't want to anchor close to the break because of the size of the swell. The surfers seemed like ants drifting in the water.

After about an hour everyone in the water was still alive, so I figured that it couldn't be too horrendous out there and I decided to paddle out. I shoulder-hopped for a while, catching the medium sized waves and getting a feel for the place. Then I caught a bigger wave or two and gained some confidence. As I was paddling back from a ride, a big set approached and although I was not in a perfect position, I decided to take a chance and I swung around for the first wave of the set. Bad idea. I came straight down with the lip and went under, luckily not hitting the bottom, but the wave would not let me go and I got jerked around under water until my lungs were empty of oxygen. Just as I was starting to panic I surfaced, but my heart sank as I saw a huge mass of white water bearing down on me, with more waves stacked up behind it. I learnt another hard lesson: don't go for the first wave of a set here if you're not certain you'll make the wave – having the rest of the set unload on your head is no fun. I had just enough time to gulp some air before the next wave hit. I tried to dive down to escape the force of the water, but I was flung forward along the surface, bodysurfing on my back for a second or two and then going through the spin cycle again. In my mind I saw myself as a cartoon character rolling down a mountain in an avalanche, flying through the air like a rag doll and getting flushed down several toilet bowls. Every now and then my feet hit the reef, so I knew I was in the shallows already, but it was impossible to gain any control over my body. I just tried to float. The third and fourth waves were slightly less powerful and slowly I managed to swim in with them. My surfboard had been snapped in two, but luckily the half that was attached to my leash was big enough to float me and eventually I made it to the beach and I retrieved the other piece. My legs were bleeding from cuts and scrapes and my board shorts had been ripped once again, but I had no major wounds and I was relieved to be alive. I paddled back to the ship slowly on my broken board, my ears burning with embarrassment and frustration. I could feel the guys in the line-up following me with their eyes and I could just hear them saying to each other, "He shouldn't have been out here. He can't handle it." On deck I licked my wounds. At least my board had a clean break and it would be possible to repair it. There were some skilled repairmen at Nias, not far away.

The following day was overcast and onshore. I was relieved that surfing was not an option and I went ashore for a beer, where I became acquainted with Vincent. Later Sean and I walked across the island and we discovered some swamps, leeches and plenty of mosquitoes. By midday we had had enough of hacking our way through spiky rattan and pulling parasites off various parts of our anatomy. It's amazing where you find leeches on your body after an hour or two in a swamp. We call them parasites, but to me leeches are really more like hunters. They sit on the leaves and branches of plants near paths and wait for suitable prey to walk past. When a warm-blooded animal approaches, the leech often stands upright on its rear end, where it holds on to the plant with a kind of suction cup. It waves its body back and forth as if smelling your scent on the air and its entire body quivers with the anticipation of a nice, warm meal. When you venture close enough, the bloodsucker launches itself through space and jumps onto you with incredible power and accuracy. Then it walks along your body by arching its back like a caterpillar until it finds a tasty spot and latches on with powerful jaws to suck voraciously. I've seen feeding leeches increase in size fourfold within minutes. Really, they are much more like lions than worms. On a recent expedition, a group of us each captured a leech and held our own Leech Olympics, consisting of a 100mm sprint, the long jump and wrestling. They performed like true athletes, especially when sprinting after a succulent outstretched hand.

To repel these nasties, people try a number of deterrents, from insect repellent, to burning cigarettes, to chilli sauce. But the only really effective way of ridding yourself of them is to check your arms and legs regularly and to pull them off as soon as they jump onto you. Where they manage to bite, they inject an anti-coagulant to keep your blood flowing freely and it can sometimes be difficult to stop the bleeding. These days, leeches are still being used in some hospitals to improve blood flow to the extremities of certain people with poor circulation.

We turned around and headed for the camp. During the lengthy slog back through the swamp, the black mud that was caked around our legs at least gave us some protection against the mosquitoes. At Vincent's we found that the beer had run out and after our long and thirsty walk, the neat rum that was on offer didn't have much appeal. Sometimes there is a very fine line between paradise and purgatory. We were grateful that we could escape to the ship.

When we came on deck, the atmosphere was very acrimonious. Gerhard and Gavin were involved in yet another argument. Apparently it had been going on for a while and we could feel the tension in the air. Gavin had just returned empty-handed form spear fishing and he stood dripping salt water, clutching his spear gun.

"No, I won't do that!" Gavin shouted at Gerhard. "If you're so set on changing things, do it yourself!" I could not work out what they were fighting about.

Gavin became increasingly agitated, stepping closer and closer to Gerhard until they were face to face. But Gerhard would not back down. He was too proud and as we all knew, he always had to win every dispute.

"Piss off, get out of my face! I am the captain and I will decide what can and cannot be done! Now go and dry off and then you start doing what you are told!"

Gavin looked like his face was going to explode. His hand mechanically reached for his water bottle, but he did not have one with him. He twisted an imaginary cap off the shank of the spear gun and fiddled with its mechanism while his eyes bored into Gerhard's. Then his features were contorted by a final paroxysm: "You know what can happen when a spear gun goes off accidentally, don't you? People can get hurt, especially you with your big head. It always gets in the way!" He glared at Gerhard once more and then stormed below.

We all stared in stunned silence. Everybody knows that you never cock a spear gun above water. It's a deadly weapon. With this outburst Gavin had gone to a place that would be very difficult to return from.

"That's it. He's gone troppo," was Jonno's remark. The rest of us were silent. We could not really argue. Whatever the cause of Gavin's distress, this outburst was the first sign that he was battling some serious storms of his own deep inside the engine room.

I went to bed early that night, but just as I was sinking into deep sleep, Richard shook me awake: "Time to pull anchor!" Another little tropical storm was buffeting the ship and we were in danger of drifting onto a reef once again. Groggily, we lined up on the slippery deck to pull the anchor rope in the rain, get the tender back on board and to stow all the loose gear so that things didn't disappear over board. After an hour's work the Explorer motored off into the night and we went back to our cabins, cursing the weather. We were starting to long for a protected anchorage like the bay at Nias, where we would have some undisturbed sleep, with no night duty or nocturnal anchor pulling. I rocked back and forth in my bunk, listening to the drone of the engine and I waited for sleep to come once more.

When Gerhard dropped anchor again, I was still awake. I checked the time and gave up on sleeping. It wasn't long until dawn. Sean, who was on duty for the last anchor watch was on deck and we sat together sipping hot chocolate while we waited for the sun. The storm had passed and with it, the chop on the water. In the dark we could make out white water on the reef, but we couldn't be sure how big the waves were or whether they were any good. I was hoping for smaller, cleaner surf than the previous day. We consulted the map and the GPS, which revealed our new location as Bawa, another little island that was known to have good waves. Again the anticipation of another surf session took hold of us. Gradually the sky became a dark purple and then slowly it turned pink before the sun came up. The offshore breeze carried a faint whiff of spices from the island and with it came the twitter of birds in the trees. Sean was already busy waking up Ron, who was on duty next, while I waxed my board. The minute Ron came on deck, Sean and I jumped into the water with our surfboards and we paddled towards the break. It was a fair distance to cover, but the surface of the ocean was smooth and the water was warm. We were fit and in good condition from surfing almost daily for the last month. Ahead of us some right-handers were peeling forever over the reef. It felt good to be alive.

The swell had moderated overnight and there were comfortable head high waves. We surfed for about an hour before a few more of the crew drifted over to join us. I had shaken off the jitters from my previous session and I was just enjoying the freedom of picking any wave I liked and enjoying the ride. It didn't matter if I fell; there was an endless supply of waves. After two and a half hours of continuous surfing my arms were getting heavy and I took my time to paddle back into the line-up. When I arrived there, the atmosphere had changed dramatically. There was a new face in the water and everyone was interested. A shapely girl in a bikini had come out from the surf camp on the island and she was surrounded by the boys from the Island Explorer, who were all very keen to give her any wave she wanted and who were all oh so polite. As she paddled back after each wave, a line of smiling guys dreamily followed closely behind her, hypnotized by her hips, smiling sweetly at her and grinning broadly at each other. As we sat behind the waves, tracing the outline of her bikini with our eyes, it was all too apparent that we had been at sea for a long time. (Although there were three women on board at this stage, they were all engaged or married and we regarded them more like sisters than sex objects.) I never learned the girl's name; she wisely declined all the invitations to come aboard for refreshments.

As I hoisted myself on deck after the session, I suddenly realised with a spasm of guilt that for the past few days I had never once thought about Anne and how she was doing back home. Not that I could do anything to communicate with her, but nevertheless, I was surprised by how easily our surroundings had managed to suck me in and to block out the exterior world. It was as if I had stepped through the looking glass, into a different dimension; into Wonderland.

It was around this time that Gerhard had managed to convince quite a few of us that the Swedish national netball team was on a ship in our vicinity for a bit of rest and relaxation. We had encountered another yacht and Gerhard had been talking to the captain on the radio. Afterwards he casually mentioned the netball team as an aside while he was talking to a few of us guys and I suppose that after being in the wilderness for so long, we really wanted to believe him. For a day or two the guys were sitting around with dreamy expressions on their faces and trying to figure out ways of meeting these tall blonde beauties. Eventually we had to let go of our fantasies of angelic Agnetha Fältskog look-alikes and face up to the fact that there was no netball team and that the yacht in question was manned by some crusty, unshaven fellows with beer bellies and bad breath.

But with or without a bevy of beauties resembling Abba's lead singers hanging around, the day was perfect: sunshine, no wind and although the swell was on the wane, it was smooth and clean. I was surfed out and after lunch I lazed around on deck, watching some of the others surf from the corner of my eye, while attempting to focus my attention enough to read a book. I woke up an hour later and flopped over board for a snorkel along a well-stocked reef. The shallows were full of brightly coloured corals, anemones and lots of reef fish. I smiled into my snorkel: the spear fishermen would be sure to come back with a good supper for us.

That evening as the sun started to set, we had sashimi straight from the sea for starters, followed by fish curry with vegetables as the main course and we washed it all down with plenty of warm Bintang beer. The company was impeccable and the conversation lively. Derek put a CD in the player and cranked it up. We played cards, told stories and speculated about Bawa and all the islands beyond. And then we had a few more beers. The night ended when some dancing got out of hand and someone almost fell overboard. After this we all agreed to go to bed. Tomorrow we would sail to Nias, home of the fabled right that has been drawing surfers for decades. And we'd see a little civilization again, and maybe even some civilized company!

The spot at Bawa was known as Fish Bowls and it was made famous by a surf video featuring Tom Curren ripping big hollow rights on a tiny surfboard. After the earthquake, the reef has shifted and Fish Bowls has never been the same since. According to people who've been back, it is now a very watered-down affair. We were lucky to have been able surf it on that day. It will probably never get that good again, at least not until the next earthquake.

Nias is just as good as they say it is in the magazines. The palm-lined point, the perfect tubes, the laid back living ashore and easy access to surf spots are all there, just like they say in the articles. Apparently it is even better now after the earthquake, faster, hollower and shallower. Whether this is really an improvement depends of course on your taste and ability. What is good for Jordy Smith and company could be a nightmare for you and me. But at the time of our visit I loved the point at Nias, because I could work on my barrel riding without worrying too much about the reef, which was relatively deep. This reef is made of lava and it's not quite as sharp as many of the coral reefs we surfed. It was a forgiving wave in the sense that if you didn't manage to ride the barrel, you wouldn't necessarily get shut out by the section and it was possible to get back onto the face of the wave and surf on.

The waves that made Nias famous break along the point in Lagundri Bay (Nias is the name of the island). Palm trees surround the settlement there and when we surfed, it was against a backdrop of greenery, making the spot even more photogenic. On a photo taken from the right angle it appears as if the surfer is riding an aquamarine wave coming straight out of the jungle. The traditional design of the wooden buildings next to the shore completes the picture of an ideal, laid back surf village in the tropics. All the ingredients required to make this one of the most idyllic surf destinations in the world are present.

The people at Lagundri were introduced to surfing many years before our visit by the legendary Australians Kevin Lovett, Peter Troy and Jon Giesel. They attained every surfer's ultimate fantasy: discovering one of the world's best waves in the most perfect surroundings. And then they surfed it all by themselves, day in and day out for weeks. No crowds, no hassles, no bad vibes in the water, just endless, wonderful waves. But before you gnaw your fingers off in frustration (because, let's face it, you are nowhere near Nias or any other good waves at the moment, otherwise you'd be surfing, not reading about it) let me give you the second part of the story. This kind of fortuity comes at a very high price. Even though the three of them must have spent countless months in planning and travelling to dead ends, while eating only rice, chillies and fish and enduring the kind of conditions that I experienced on my bus ride constantly for weeks, that was still not enough payment for what they were about to receive.

Six months after discovering Nias, Jon Giesel was dead. He got malaria and then pneumonia, from which he never recovered. Life out here is deadly.

The level of surfing amongst the locals was very high. Of course they knew the break inside out and they had the chance to surf one of the world's prime waves on a regular basis, year in and year out. On more than one occasion I saw a wave coming and considered paddling for it, only to realize that there was already a local surfer on the wave, deep inside the tube, having taken off way behind the section, back-dooring the barrel and gunning all the way through to where the wave slowed down. If these guys ever get to go on a surf trip, they're bound to be disappointed; very few places can compete with Lagundri. It will either be too cold, too windy or the waves won't measure up to what they have at home.

Paradoxically, locals on many islands with perfect surf struggle to learn, because the only waves they have are death barrels over razor reefs. When you think about it, it is much easier to learn to surf at a weak beach break with poor waves than at most of the serious surf spots. Here in Lagundri there was a smaller, less powerful reform wave in the shallows, which allowed the kids to learn the basics and build confidence before paddling to the outside wave. The constant stream of travelling surfers and pros that visited kept them up to speed with developments in board design and technique, so the local kids were motivated and fit to surf.

Sorake Beach is the name of the village that developed on the shore where the waves rifle off. There were houses along the point where most surfers who travelled over land found accommodation and where I stopped to have my broken board repaired. Further along there were a few informal shops in people's homes that sold basic goods like soap and food. I bought a whole lot of fruit: bunches of bananas still on the chopped-off branch, green as well as dried coconuts and some huge, sugary sweet pineapples. As I strolled around the settlement, I thought how lucky the people here were that tacky department stores, branded goods shops and of course McDonalds hadn't reached them yet (but I suspect that they might just disagree with me). There were three little restaurants serving tasty dishes, banana or papaya shakes and coconut milk. It was great to have a change from the ship's food and we spent a lot of time sipping iced drinks on the porches, out of the hot sun. A few of us swallowed hard when, after placing an order for chicken satay, we saw a boy running off down the street and returning with a live chicken under his arm. A few squawks later we had large plates full of fresh chicken in front of us. "At least the poor bugger would have had a happy life. Scratching around for food between the houses with all its friends and sleeping under a roof at night can't be all that bad," remarked Francois. "When the chop came, it was swift."

"Mmm," Ron had his mouth full. "Better than the lives of most chickens in the West. Everybody at Lagundri has it good, even the chickens."

It was refreshing to be able to walk around on land and to see different people for a change. I got onto the back of a 50cc bike with a local named Ketut and we buzzed off on a white-knuckle ride (without a helmet, of course) to the nearby town of Teluk Dalam. Ketut kept a ghetto blaster, with the volume turned up full tilt, balanced on his lap through all the turns, bumps and potholes. He dropped me off in front of an internet café in a dazed state and with ringing ears.

As I sat down in front of a rather dilapidated computer, an Australian in the back gesticulated at his console and asked, "Hey, does this thing with electricity?" The connection wasn't good. Downloading just a short e-mail took forever and if you accidentally clicked on the wrong thing, you had to start all over again. I spent half an hour staring at the passersby in the street, while waiting for my e-mail account to open up, only to get a rather disheartening series of letters from Anne, upbeat in the beginning – "Hope to hear from you soon. All my love, Anne" – gradually degenerating into, "Where are you cavorting around now?", then, "When are you going to think of letting me know you are still alive?" and finally a plaintive, "Please let me know you're ok."

I felt terrible about Anne's distress, but there had been no way of contacting her in the time that we had been sailing through the islands south of Nias. Luckily, we were going to stay anchored in Lagundri for a number of days and I would be able to phone Anne up and put her mind at rest during that period. But I knew that we'd be moving on again and who knows where we'd end up? I sent her an e-mail to try to reassure her and said that I'd phone later that day, and then I braved the streets of Teluk Dalam again.

Being the only white face in town meant a fair amount of attention for me and along with it, the usual guides and touts. The kids in the street took turns chanting "Hello Mister" at me non-stop and as soon as one trader with a tray of fake merchandise left my side, another one took his place. After an hour I could fluently say in Indonesian, "No thank you, I do not need a new watch / sarong / back-scratcher / girlfriend / your sister." It was a relief to see Ketut returning on his fifty and the ride back was much more bearable knowing that I was leaving Hellomisterville.

On my arrival back in Sorake Beach I met a British girl who had heard that there were doctors on board our ship. She had cut her ankle while walking on the reef a week previously and was now worried about it. I took one look at the bloated leg and told her to get to a hospital as soon as she could. Cellulitis had set in and the skin was red, pock marked and weeping pus. I could not make out her ankle because of all the swelling. We had oral antibiotics on board, but they would not be effective against infection that was this far advanced. The closest good hospital was in Singapore – a ferry crossing, a hectic bus ride and then a flight away. It would take at least two days of travelling if she was very lucky; more likely three or four days. But she was reluctant to accept my advice. After all, it had taken her a long time to get to Nias and she did not want to spoil her holiday. I tried to reason with her, explaining the seriousness of the situation and that her leg might have to be amputated if the infection got worse. She said she would think about it. All I could do was to give her some antibiotic pills and to urge her once more to get proper treatment, but she stayed on and we spotted her hobbling around the village over the following few days. I wonder now whether she still has her leg and whether Nias (or maybe his name was something like Ketut) was worth losing a limb over.

It seems that not many people came to Lagundri by boat at the time of our visit. Most surfers travelled across Sumatra and took a ferry to Nias from there. They stayed in the houses along the point and many families had come to depend on these lodgers for an income. I suppose it's understandable then that the locals were unhappy with us who arrived on their shore and surfed their waves, but did not spend money locally on accommodation. We started to get dirty looks in the water and people began to drop in on our waves. At first we could not understand what was causing this hostility. Arguments started in the line-up and at one stage the unpleasantness almost deteriorated to violence. I remember sitting on the shoulder and watching Sean take off on a good-sized wave. The next moment a local took a late drop into the wave just ahead of him, falling out of the sky almost on top of him and narrowly missing Sean's head with his board. Somehow Sean managed to stay upright and ride to safety, but the incident and the shouting match that followed it spoiled the session and the day completely. Something had to be done and Gerhard and Francois went to speak to some of the local representatives. They explained that we wouldn't be staying for long and that some of us had in fact slept in some of the local losmens for a change of scenery and for some privacy. We had eaten in the restaurants on most evenings. This helped matters, but I never really felt comfortable in the water again after those incidents.

On our last morning at Nias my internal clock woke me before first light. In the dark I pulled on some boardshorts, tiptoed to the bow to get my surfboard and slipped over the side of the ship into the black water, trying not to make a splash. I did not want anyone on board to wake up and join me in the surf. I wanted to be alone out there. The water was warmer than the early morning air and it felt like I was paddling through a warm bath as I made my way over to the break in the murk. I arrived at the take-off spot just as the horizon started to brighten up. Even at that time I wasn't the first one out. One of the guys from a losmen on the water's edge was sitting on his board, waiting for the first wave of the day. We sat together in silence. It was quiet between sets, there was not a breath of wind and the water was slick and dark, like oil. As the horizon started to turn orange, a set approached. The first wave went to the other guy, and then it was my turn. I pushed my board down my wave in the half-light and got to my feet. I couldn't see much; I felt my way along the face of the wave, just taking in the near weightlessness and the smoothness of the water. The lip curled over me and for a second or two I was crouched in the tube, listening to the rush of the sea around me in the darkness. The next moment I was under water as the wave closed out, my ride over – but I surfaced with a smile. I paddled back to the ship soon after this wave. This was how I wanted to remember Nias.

When I went ashore to pick up my repaired surfboard later that morning, I heard the news that an American boat captain who had been based in Lagundri and who was married to a local girl had died the previous night. It was malaria. He had had the infection before and he knew the symptoms. When he felt a fever coming on earlier that week, he went to bed to sweat it out as usual. He never got up again. This was a stark reminder that we were not invincible. All of us on the Explorer were becoming complacent when it came to malaria prophylaxis. Although our risk of being bitten by mosquitoes was a lot less out on the water than what it would have been on land, the chance of contracting malaria was always there. And it's deadly. Again I was reminded of the thin line separating the fantasy we were living from total disaster. We were all sobered by the news.

Thinking back on it now, I find it strange that, although I sometimes lay awake at night, I never really worried about things at the time. We were on an adventure and the only important things to most of us were whether we would find waves the next day, what they would be like and where they were. And, of course, what's for supper! We didn't think too far ahead and even if we did worry about what was going on back at home, it was impossible to find out what was happening there. We had no way of communicating with the outside world until we arrived in the next major port. So we lived in the present and we concerned ourselves only with the day-to-day things that we could change. If a storm came or the engine gave trouble, we would deal with it when the problem arose. I think that if only everyone in the world could find that frame of mind now, it would be a much happier place. Obviously, things were different for Gerhard, Charmaine, Gavin and the other partners who had to take more responsibility. There were also the worries about accidents at sea, running aground, sinking and even pirates. We had no way of getting help other than by using emergency flares and the ship's radio, which in this remote area were of questionable value. But why worry about things you can't change?

After a week on Nias it was good to be on our way again. We were headed for Aceh province and the northern tip of Sumatra. I had read in a guidebook that there were some known surf spots in the north and I was looking forward to seeing new places. But before I could enjoy the waves and the sights of the Indian Ocean again, there was a price to pay to Neptune. Soon after we left the shelter of Lagundri Bay, we were hit by strong winds and heaving swells. I quickly became queasy again. By this time I had hoped that I would have found my sea legs, but the rolling of the ship was too much for me. I was not the only one, but when the going got tough, I was the sickest. Motion sickness tablets, ginger pills, pressure bracelets and acupuncture were all of no benefit to me. The only thing that helped was sleep, so I spent a lot of time in my bunk. When the sea was very rough I was almost completely incapacitated, but most of the time at least I managed to do my duties on deck. Steering the ship did help the nausea, but it is surprisingly difficult to keep a vessel on course at sea, especially when the weather is bad. There is a delay between when the wheel is turned, the rudder tilts and any effect on the course of the ship is noticeable. An inexperienced helmsman might turn the wheel and, not seeing any change in course, turn it some more. The ship now veers off to one side and he has to make a correction in the opposite direction, with similar results again. A seagull looking down on the ship from high up while I was steering would have seen us doing some interesting manoeuvres including zigzags, S-curves and the odd roundhouse cutback every now and then. When we entered busy shipping lanes, I preferred to leave the wheel to somebody else. Trying to avoid huge freighters while fighting with steering that functioned according to a completely obscure set of rules felt like drunk-driving a donkey cart down the wrong side of a highway full of 18-wheeler trucks.In view of the bad weather, we decided to abandon local exploration and the course was set for the island of Sabang, just off Sumatra's northern-most shore. We were heading for the Andaman Sea. We were now entering pirate territory. The Straits of Malacca must be one of the world's original pirate haunts. Ever since the Bugis people of Sulawesi started sailing these shores in ships like ours almost a millennium ago, sea captains and sailors have been nervous when they passed through the Straits. This gateway between the trade routes of Arabia and India to the west and the Far East on the other side has always been a great place for a buccaneer, because large volumes of sea traffic have to move through this narrow bottleneck. But it was the spice trade that really added zing to local affairs. For many centuries the Banda Islands in the Malukus were the world's only source of mace and nutmeg. There are records of trade between China and the Bandanese Islands dating back to Roman times. By the 1200's Arab merchants were sailing through the Malaccan Straits to reach the major trading ports in Indonesia for access to the all-important spices. Mace, nutmeg and cloves formed the backbone of the economy in these parts. Many a sultan lived extremely well on the proceeds of the spice trade. And wherever there are lots of ships creaking under the weight of their extremely valuable cargoes, there will be pirates. When the Portuguese finally found a route to the spice-islands in the 1500's, closely followed by the Dutch, the English and the Spanish, the increase in trade gave piracy here the shot in the arm that made it notorious until today.

I remember playing with a bottle of cloves as a child, taking in that strong, sweet aroma and pushing the hard black cloves into an orange as if they were nails. I did not realize then that they had once been pretty little flowers. The label on the bottle had a picture of an ancient sailing ship and I was fascinated by where that ship must have gone to collect its cargo. A whole fantasy world comprising everybody from Sinbad the Sailor to Captain Hook still exists for me in one of those bottles. Thinking of the warm Indian Ocean filled with colourful characters from a bygone era of sailing ships, treasure chests and swashbuckling buccaneers makes me want to drop everything, grab a cutlass and head for the nearest recruiting inn at the harbour. I know that actually pirates are nothing but thieves, thugs and common criminals, but if I had to be a murdering fugitive, I'd choose to be a pirate in the age of sail.

Today the Straits continue to shelter modern-day pirates. The coast of Sumatra is undeveloped and it offers many good hiding places in its numerous hidden bays and little offshore islands. Nowadays pirates are equipped with speedboats, AK-47's and radar. Even huge oil tankers have vanished without a trace from here. According to a documentary that I watched on television, the pirates board the tanker at night, shoot the crew while they are sleeping and dump them over board. The crews on the tankers are small, as most operations aboard these ships are automated. The tanker is then renamed and false papers are secured in a country where it is possible to bribe officials. Voila, you now possess a floating industrial zone worth many millions. Nabbing mega freighters is a lucrative business, but there are risks. I read recently that a high-ranking Chinese bureaucrat had been executed for corruption relating to this kind of affair.

Our ship was small fry and was probably of little interest to pirates, but you never know what they might get up to. We kept our eyes peeled.

The Island Explorer kept plodding ahead through the rough seas at an average speed of about four knots, increasing to a maximum of eight knots when we were surfing down big swells with the wind from behind (i.e. we weren't moving that much faster than you can paddle in a kayak) for the next two days. I spent my time feeding the fish over the side of the ship or lying passed out in my bunk and the others played cards, read, argued disinterestedly or just stared into space, also green at the gills. Most of the time there was nothing to see but swells, white caps and a smudged horizon. The food was crap, because it's hell to cook in a galley where everything is sliding (or bouncing) around constantly – plates leap out of cupboards that are left unsecured and boiling pots threaten to up-end themselves over the cook. At mealtimes we could look forward to dry biscuits and Beng-Bengs, with canned sardines in tomato sauce for those who had the stomach. I recommend a cruise aboard a small ship on the open ocean to anybody who needs to lose weight fast. With the weather remaining bad, we carried on motoring north, trying to make as much progress as we could. In my bunk I closed my eyes and transported myself to better places with sunshine, drinks with little umbrellas in them and bikini clad girls playing ukuleles.

Derek said that he became accustomed to killing time like this after a stint of work he had done in Kazakhstan. He had worked as a co-ordinator for a medical evacuation company in a remote mining area. So when a mineshaft collapsed or some similar disaster occurred, he would be rushing around like a headless chicken, but mostly he sat around doing nothing, just waiting. You could describe it as boredom punctuated by panic, to borrow an expression from Samuel Shem. (He was referring to anaesthetists.)

Derek is a very likeable, social person, the kind of guy who puts everybody at ease and who keeps a conversation flowing easily, with lots of laughs thrown in. I always enjoyed spending time around him, because he was upbeat and he lifted everyone's spirits. He was also a great nudist, one of his qualities that were less appreciated on board. There were many times when you would hear someone exclaim, "Aw Derek, put some pants on man! Not at the breakfast table!" And then you would see him dive over the side with his legs spread open for balance, or maybe for extra effect.

The thing that kept Derek sane in Kazakhstan was that, presumably because a lot of doctors from South Africa worked there, they could watch South African television in the doctors' mess. What captivated his Kazakhstani colleagues was the rugby. Derek is a big rugby fan and he watched match after match. The sport is completely unknown in Kazakhstan, but its macho nature, obscure set of rules and the grunting of the players in the scrums appealed to the locals. He soon converted several guys and they all followed the Curry Cup competition avidly. Apparently, what they really liked was that the forwards wound lots of duct tape around their heads and then proceeded to bash into each other repeatedly head first. (At this time scrumcaps were not widely used and it was a fairly regular occurrence to see the field assistants taping up heads during stoppage time as if they were repairing split open skulls.) You can just imagine the talk on the field: "There you are Buks, right as rain again. We'll bolt the two halves together properly after the game. Now go and ram that number two off the pitch!"

After what seemed like an eternity, the wind gradually died

down and the sun came out. Most importantly, the sea calmed down and by the middle of the day we were drifting on silky smooth dark blue water under clear skies, with bright white clouds high above. Our ship had rounded Sumatra and we found ourselves in the relatively protected water of the Malaccan Strait. When we looked down into the depths, it felt like we were staring into infinity. It seemed as if there was no end to the blue vastness. We stopped the ship's engine and lowered the ladder on the side of the ship. The Island Explorer drifted in the quietness of the Ocean, with nothing except water around it.

We all went for a swim, drifting alongside the ship, staring into the clear water below us and after a while we turned around and floated on our backs. We watched the clouds as they slowly built themselves into castles in the sky and then broke up into separate pieces again. I swam deep down, blew air from my lungs and followed the silver bubbles as they rose upwards. They expanded as they came closer to the surface, becoming bigger and bigger before bursting into the atmosphere again. Once more I lay on the surface face down, peering into a different world. Looking down through the translucent water into the depths made me feel giddy, as if I was suspended high up in the sky, gliding through empty space. The ocean floor was probably several kilometres deep here and every now and then I had the sensation that I was falling into the nothingness, like in a dream. Eventually we had to climb back on board again and reconnect with our world, but that surreal experience in the water stayed with me for a long time afterwards. We continued to sail onwards towards Malaysia.

It became oppressively hot that night and I was lying in a pool of sweat in my bunk. The plastic mattress cover was sticking to my skin and it felt like I was in a sauna. My cabin was right next to the engine room and the diesel engine was radiating heat like a furnace, baking me slowly in my berth. The sea was calm, with no chop on the surface and we were gliding along smoothly through the night, so I opened my porthole to let in some cool air. A light breeze blew in, carrying the salty smell of the sea and at last I fell into a dreamy sleep.

In my dream I was coming out of a crystal clear barrel, flying onto the shoulder of the wave and drawing a perfect arc back into the pocket. But, as I was setting up for a powerful lip bash, the water came up to meet me and I was hit full in the face by a tub-full of salty sea, knocking all the air from my lungs. It felt like a big, angry man had slapped me really hard. Water was streaming through the open porthole and all over my cabin, soaking everything. I lay back gasping in the puddle that my bunk had become, laughing and still out of breath from the wave that chose to jump through the window to visit me in my dream.

The following morning dawned clear and fresh, with a moderate wind blowing from behind the Island Explorer and a clean swell running with the ship. Gerhard was in good spirits, full of energy and enterprise: "What do you boys say we hoist sails and give this baby a go? Let's see what she can do."

He stood in front of the wheelhouse like a sea captain in the days of yore, as the rest of us ran around on deck, getting into our positions. "Away, my merry sailor men! Loose the sails and brace the yards!" and we unfastened the ties that held the canvass. The sails rumbled and shook in the breeze as we tugged on the ropes. Francois and Richard went up the rigging, out onto the yardarms and as the ship swayed with the swell, they rocked back and forth like macaques in a palm tree. Gerhard shouted out more instructions and the wind filled the sails with a loud crack. They bulged forward and the Explorer surged ahead. The ketch glided smoothly over the sea and powered over the swells. We felt like real old salts as we sat on the foredeck and felt the planks under our feet trill with the motion of the ship. Ahead of us lay the endless ocean and beyond it, Malaysia. I stared at the water whizzing past below me, mesmerized by the smooth motion of the ship and I completely forgot about any seasickness I might have had. For a while some dolphins swam with the ship, riding the bow wave and then they disappeared again, effortlessly moving ahead of the ship. Flying fish were also breaking the surface regularly and we kept a sharp look-out for any that might fall onto the deck; food was never far from our thoughts. Unfortunately the Explorer rode too high out of the water for them to reach.

The favourable winds lasted for most of the day and we kept the sails up, making good headway. The Explorer forged ahead across the trackless deep.

After another two days we started to near Langkawi, a group of islands off the west coast of Malaysia near the country's border with Thailand. One morning I came on deck at first light and I saw an enchanting world before me, completely different from the islands that we had been sailing past along the Sumatran coast. There were small limestone outcrops jutting out of the shallow sea everywhere around us, measuring about ten to twenty metres in diameter. Each mini-island had vertical cliffs where the sea had eroded the stone away, creating striking pillars, overhangs and caves in the rock. It was as if we were gliding past a fantasy world made by a wild imagination. There were dozens of islets shaped like mushrooms where the waves had scoured away the rock at their bases. They were covered with green trees, creepers and ferns. Birds of every kind and colour circled these rocky platforms constantly. They nested on the cliffs, under overhangs and in the trees and there was a never-ending display of diving into the sea as they searched for fish. Gradually the sun rose and it turned the sky into a succession of exotic hues, reflected in the mirror-like water that we were gliding through. There was no wind and the air around us was filled with bird cries. The only hint that civilisation was not far away was an occasional ship's horn sounding in the distance. Some small fishing boats put-putted past us, occupied by one or two fishermen wearing pointed palm frond hats and each of them had a trained cormorant sitting at the helm of the boat, eyeing the water for fish. Apart from the small outboard motors on the boats, this scene could not have changed much in the last few hundred years. It was as if we had sailed back in time, to an era when life stirred at a slow pace, when people moved to a different rhythm. It was beautiful. No one on deck said a word. The atmosphere was almost spiritual, like we were experiencing some religious revelation and it was deeply humbling. I wished that we could continue to drift through that scene forever and I tried to capture the experience in my mind exactly so that I could remember it just as it was forever. It's only a vague memory now, a pang of longing.

As we approached Lankawi's major port, it was my turn at the helm. I nervously held onto the large wooden wheel, keeping the spokes lined up with little marks on the wood panelling in front of it, so that we didn't accidentally veer off course. There was a lot of traffic near the harbour and I did not want any close calls with other ships. Gavin said that he would take over from me as soon as he had adjusted something below. As he left the wheelhouse he said something over his shoulder, but I couldn't hear him and I let him go. Moments later Gavin came roaring up the stairs, swearing like a proper sailor, crimson in the face. "Didn't I just fucking tell you not to fucking touch the fucking choke, whatever you fucking do, you fucking Japie?"

I just stared at him, dumbfounded. I don't think I even knew that there was a choke lever. From the corner of my eye I now saw black smoke billowing from the exhaust.

I still don't think that I had anything to do with what went wrong below, but I let Gavin rant until he got it all out of his system and then I let him take the wheel. Later that day he quietly apologised to me. He was clearly struggling to maintain control of himself. I wondered how long he would be able to hold out.

What a contrast the town of Langkawi itself was to the waters in which it was situated. It had been developed extensively, with a modern (if small) business district, hotels, good infrastructure and an airport. There were many yachts and flashy speedboats in the harbour. Everything was well ordered and it was not necessary to bribe harbour officials for access to basic amenities.

After we had berthed in the harbour, a group of us walked into town. There were billboards with pictures of everything in the vicinity: the coast, the hills, the sea and everything in it. I presume these images were for the benefit of those who did not want to leave their resorts to go and look for themselves. There were plastic models of the limestone islands, with rubber palm trees and luminescent plastic ferns. Rubber snakes and plastic fish eagles tried to look lifelike on the road verges. It was as if the local authorities did not think that the tourists they were trying to attract would notice these things without helpful hints around every corner. Big hotels, with even bigger advertising boards lined the road from the harbour. Brand new taxis were transporting tourists in floral shirts and Bermuda shorts to flashy shops while busses were picking up touring parties to go and swim with dolphins or to watch seals jump through hoops at the local water park. For every natural attraction near the town there was an artificial scaled down replica along a road somewhere. It reminded me of the people back home who build swimming pools on their properties right next to the sea. Why would you ever want to swim in that restricted little chlorine-filled imitation when you have the entire ocean right there on your doorstep in all its splendour? But the important thing about Langkawi was that the port had good facilities for doing repairs to our ship. Some of our minor engine problems were becoming more and more difficult to deal with at sea and now they had to be fixed properly.

While Gavin and Ron started working on the engine, the rest of us had some expensive fast food at the Malaysian equivalent of KFC. I managed to locate an internet café for an update from home. Anne mentioned in one of her letters that Hansie Cronje, the squeaky clean South African cricket captain, had admitted to match fixing. I'm not a big cricket fan, but I was familiar with the media's picture of the captain and his wholesome family values, humble but strong attitude and stalwart Christian character. My first reaction to the news was "No, there was some sort of mistake. Not Hansie!"

"Not Hansie!" I heard the exclamation when I came around a street corner. André and Francois were telling an incredulous Sean the news. They had obviously also seen it on the net somewhere. As I climbed up the ladder of our ship, I heard it again, "Not Hansie!" Derek and Melissa were the next to hear the story. Ron, being a Kiwi, enjoyed the whole episode immensely. "Not Hansie!" he crowed over and over again.

We looked at branded goods in the shop windows and walked around town for a while, but we soon ran out of things to do. Richard and Francois had been sent to obtain parts for the ship's engine and Gavin stayed in the engine room permanently, only coming on deck for meals and to sleep, covering everything he touched in grease. I was glad that I knew nothing about machines. I imagine that when naughty mechanics die they will be sent to a place where they spend their days in an unventilated engine room, anchored deep in the tropics.

In the meantime, the rest of us had to kill time in Malaysia's artificial version of itself and it was very boring. Gerhard and Charmaine were buying plane tickets back to Cape Town. After building a ship for more than a year and then sailing it to our current position, they said they needed a break. Pete was joining them. There were also stories that there were financial issues that had to be sorted out urgently from back home. A ship does not just stay afloat automatically and there were ongoing expenses. But we all speculated about the spear gun incident and the effect that it had on Gerhard and his decision to leave. Nobody likes to have a lethal weapon waved in their face accompanied by thinly veiled threats. However, it did feel a little as if Gerhard and Charmaine were abandoning us to the whims of somebody who did not always appear to be playing with a full deck of cards.

Whatever the undercurrents on our ship were, I resolved not to worry about them. I was sailing in one of the best parts of the world and nothing else mattered very much.

Of course this new turn of events meant that Gavin had been promoted from first mate to captain. I hoped that he would feel more relaxed now that he could do things the way he preferred to. While Gerhard was in charge, he ran the ship in a fairly autocratic way, making most of the final decisions himself. He did consult with people on board about what we wanted to do, but in the end he was the captain and, much like the skippers of the military ships of years gone by, he did not allow anyone to dictate to him.

We now entered a more democratic phase, where things would be put to a vote if there was disagreement about the way forward. Gavin still had the final word, but generally he followed the outcome of the vote. This was very much as the pirates of old would have operated. Pirate ships, by the way, were of the first documented democratic institutions in the world. Long before the constitution of the United States was written, or the French Revolution took place, pirates voted amongst themselves on matters of importance. You can just imagine a band of rough, desperate seamen gathering on deck, clamouring and shouting while their captain climbs onto a sea chest and then roars, "Shall we make him walk the plank, me hearties? All those in favour, say aye!"

After a few days of mooching on some of the local beaches and drinking cold Tiger beers (a nice change), we said goodbye to Gerhard and Charmaine and we left the Langkawi theme park. It did indeed look as if a weight had been lifted from Gavin's shoulders as we streamed out of the harbour.

As luck would have it, yet again a first class storm was hovering off the coast, just waiting for us to leave the protection of the placid waters of Langkawi. For a very brief period we tried to run before it, but to no avail. The Island Explorer might have been incredibly romantic, but it had never been fast. As the wind caught up with us, I could hear its raucous laugh as it churned the sea into a maelstrom again. I think I heard my name echoing around the ship as the waves slapped the hull and I knew the sea had it in for me personally. I resigned myself to my bunk once more.

The storm was short but sharp and it washed us northwards into Thailand. This time all Gavin's work on the engine was undone in one hellish night and eventually we limped into the harbour at Phuket Island.

Patong Beach, the main town on Phuket, is the first stop on countless package tours and honeymoon trips to Thailand. Why tour operators would think that newlywed couples would want to come to Patong is beyond me. The town was basically one big whorehouse, filled with prostitutes of every imaginable kind: male, female and several intermediate stages as well. Everything was on offer, from massages to stage shows to long-term relationships. You could see middle aged European men walking around town with their Thai "girlfriends", visiting restaurants, going to the beach and so on. This arrangement would last for two or three weeks until the end of the holiday, when Claus would fly back to Germany and Nigel from London would take his place a day or two later.

Outside Patong Beach there were some respectable hotels where the honeymoon couples stayed and this was where Derek and Melissa went for a break away from their cabin. The boys left them to their own devices and went out for a night on the town.

At night you don't so much walk in Patong Beach as pick your way among the prostitutes. The moment we stepped out of our taxi, we were accosted by several women with various propositions, promises and predictions about the evening. They complimented us on our good looks, grabbed us, groped us and tried to pull us into doorways. At one point we had to drag Ron down a staircase where he was being smothered by several ladies of varying degrees of femininity (some of them had moustaches). I must admit, we did feel like rock stars and it was great walking down the street and getting the royal treatment from everybody. If you could ignore the fact that every other male tourist in town was getting the same amount of attention, it was a brilliant ego boost. After checking out the scene for a while, we attended a cabaret with very little singing or music, but with some interesting dancing and some fascinating displays of skill by the performers. Without going into too much detail, I can say that some of the ladies were fantastic shots with a blowpipe, hitting balloons with darts from a good distance and not once using their mouths. This beats the famous ping-pong ball trick hands down.

After the cabaret everything else seemed a little insipid, so we spent the rest of the evening drinking beer and dancing at a dodgy club. The only way to be fairly certain that you were dancing with a woman was to pick the ugly, plump girls. The real lookers always turned out to be gender-bending boys.

Later I watched the dawn from the main beach. A team of cleaners picked up the previous day's litter and they were followed by some men with metal detectors, scratching in the sand for lost jewellery. Soon the first sunbathers of the day arrived, still crimson from the previous day's exposure. They moved their rented deck chairs into place, lathered on sunscreen and started flipping through copies of People magazine and cheap paperbacks. They smoked and chewed gum and every now and then they would laugh lecherously, but they never smiled. Cool-drink vendors started to patrol back and forth between them and curio sellers unpacked their wares. The lady offering traditional Thai massages opened her stall.

At first I couldn't work out what was wrong with this beach scene, what it was that I was missing, but then I realized that I wanted to see children building sand castles or playing in rock pools. I wanted to see people searching for seashells in the shallows, not using metal detectors to find bracelets and diamond rings. Here there were only bloated men with multiple body piercings and tattoos, and hard looking bottle blond women wearing g-strings. Everything, including the beach, seemed to be for adults only.

Sean and I rented a scooter and got the hell out of there. We headed inland, for the hills.

The scooter came with one helmet. There was no option of renting a second one, but Sean said he didn't mind; he disliked helmets anyway. So I sat on the back, wearing the helmet and we started zig-zagging up the slopes outside Patong Beach, the breeze giving us some welcome respite from the hot air in town. But soon a motorcycle cop (without a helmet) overtook us and made us pull over. He looked forbidding, with one-way shades and the obligatory moustache. How can Sean be so reckless and not wear a helmet, he wanted to know. Sean, being a very diplomatic kind of guy, did not point out that the police officer himself was not wearing one. Instead he explained that we could only rent one helmet and that I had chosen to wear it. The lawman was aware that it was not possible to rent two helmets, but he was still very upset that Sean could be helmetless. Surely it was obvious to everybody that the person in control of the bike should wear protective headgear, not the passenger. After I gave Sean the helmet, the officer let us go with a warning, shaking his head, "Tourists …"

The road wound up the hill, affording glimpses of the coastline below through the trees. As I glanced down, I saw waves breaking along a stretch of beach and there was a surfboard lying on the sand. Suddenly I was anxious. We could be missing out on some waves! Phuket is not known for its surf, so we did not even consider looking for waves, but here there was evidence that we could be wrong. The storm that had driven us here could have brought surf and we could not bear the thought of forgoing a decent session. It had been a long time since our last surf in Nias. Sean stopped the bike and we peered down through the vegetation, taking a good look at the little beach below us. No, it was onshore and no bigger than a foot and a half. The surfboard was there more for show than anything else. We relaxed and continued our ride.

At a little roadside stall we had rice for breakfast, just as spicy as in Indonesia, but with a different taste. The underlying flavours were lighter and subtler, with lemongrass and ginger and some other aromas that we didn't know. We sat on the ground and chewed our food in silence, smiling over at the elderly lady who had sold us the rice and she smiled back at us, unable to communicate in any other way. Once again we were in a new land with its own culture and quirks and once again I got a kick out of discovering them.

The other very obvious difference here was the writing. The Thai alphabet is completely different from anything we knew, so it was impossible to read anything, most importantly road signs. In the West, even in countries where one cannot understand the language, one can usually still read place names, so finding the way remains relatively easy. Here we were completely in the dark about where we were going. This was fine initially, because we were heading out into the countryside, just putting some distance between the town and ourselves. We decided not to worry about finding our way back just yet.

Compared to Sumatra, this area had a very different feel. Instead of mosques and minarets, we saw Buddhist shrines. The buildings were usually smaller and more discreet than those of the Muslims that we had seen in Indonesia, but here there were lots of gold coloured carvings and statues with bold red, pink and yellow colours everywhere. There were flowers and smouldering incense sticks in the shrines, with statues of the Buddha in different poses and sizes. I found these shrines so much happier and more welcoming than the mosques with their many rules. There was a sense of fun without being frivolous or superficial.

Sean came and sat down next to me outside the little temple we had just visited.

"They don't seem to take themselves as seriously as the other major religions, do they?"

"You mean the Buddhists?"

"Yes, they seem so much more open to new ideas and

different opinions. They aren't so dogmatic; they will happily talk to you and listen to your views without trying to convert you."

"Ja, they make all that petty squabbling over minor differences amongst the other religions seem so childish."

"Just like kids bickering amongst each other about who is right or wrong."

"Ja bru, we can learn from that. We aren't always right about everything we believe."

Everywhere people were friendly and helpful without demanding payment for every little favour. They gave us food and drinks without asking for money and they seemed genuinely interested in who we were and where we were going. The problems seemed to arise when Western culture and local customs met, like at Patong Beach. Compared to the countryside, that place was like Sodom and Gomorrah, utterly different from what we were experiencing just a few kilometres inland. People were friendly and helpful up there and they seemed contented and at peace with their surroundings.

The day passed quickly and after visiting a few villages, looking at beautiful wood carvings that were just too big to take home with us and getting thoroughly lost, we eventually arrived back where we started that morning, but feeling like different people. We declined the offers for ficky-fick and sucky-suck, ignored the girls who told us how long they would love us and we went back to the harbour to meditate in our cabins on Phuket's split personality.

The Explorer spent another day in the harbour until Gavin managed to acquire the necessary parts for engine repairs and then, with some temporary restoration done, we set off for Koh Phi Phi Don, the larger of two picture perfect islands not far from Phuket. Koh Phi Phi was a more pleasant setting in which to spend our time and there were still some rudimentary resources that could be used if we did need spare parts or tools.

The Andaman Sea is quite sheltered from wave action in this area and we managed to cover the short distance without incident.

The approach to Koh Phi Phi is over shallow, cobalt-coloured water dotted by innumerable little green islets. Next to one of these small limestone fortresses a small yacht was swaying slowly at her anchor. We hove too next to her and said hello on the radio. After a minute, a shapely lady came on deck. Her blond hair hung loose, down to the small of her back and she had a wonderful all-over tan. She waved and gave us a nervous smile, but none of the guys on the Explorer noticed her bright white teeth or the expression on her face. Their eyes remained fixed somewhat lower down – the only thing she was wearing was a string of ivory coloured shells around her neck. For a while we stared at each other in silence and then she gave a little start of surprise. "So sorry," she said, "I forgot I wasn't wearing any clothes!" She picked up a sarong and draped it around her. Sean swallowed audibly, walked away to the opposite side of the ship muttering, "Excuse me, I need a cold shower urgently." With that, he dove into the water and started swimming briskly. Gavin, as the captain, had spoken to our new acquaintance on the radio and he now said hello hesitantly. We all tried to make small talk, feeling rather awkward. Lola was from Spain, but she spoke good English. After a while, she shouted something in Spanish and her partner, Javier came to say hello as well, causing a stir all over again. He had the same dress sense as Lola's, making everybody uncomfortable all over again and maybe a little envious. He quickly grabbed a sarong as well.

"We have been sailing around the world for the last year," Lola said. "Mostly we have stayed away from the busy ports and we keep to ourselves. It's been such a long time; we're not sure how to deal with lots of people any more. The books we have with us all say that these islands are too beautiful to miss, so we sailed here and it is really wonderful. But we feel unsure about going to Koh Phi Phi, with so many people there."

"Oh, everybody is so laid back in these parts, anything goes," Francois said. "You'll be fine."

"You don't understand; we haven't been on settled land for three months and the last time was in such a remote place that the local people spoke no language that we knew. We were actually relieved. Now we have to face crowds of people all at once, many of them Westerners like you, some may even be Spanish. I don't know what we will say to them. We are not used to humanity anymore."

There was little that we could talk about with Lola and Javier; their values and points of reference had changed and we could make no connection with them. They were friendly and eager for company in a certain sense, but at the same time they were unable to relate to us. They had departed from the life the rest of us knew. Now they lived in a parallel universe, only linking up to our world when there was no alternative. They had really dropped off the map.

"Well, we have to get going," Gavin said after a while. "See you on the island in a day or two; maybe we'll have a drink …" But we all knew that was not going to happen. We never did see them on Koh Phi Phi.

To me Koh Phi Phi was more beautiful than any of the islands we had visited before. The bigger island was shaped like an apple core, consisting of two striking half moons of white sand on either side of the island, forming shallow bays in which several yachts were anchored. A narrow isthmus of land separated the bays, with a larger area on one side where the village was located. Purple bougainvillea plants seemed to grow everywhere, making it look like the island had just been decorated for some festival. The placid waters surrounding the island were as clear as seawater can be, with a light blue colour from afar. If you climbed to the highest point on Phi Phi Don, you could look down on this smooth blue canvass and see the long white arcs drawn by motorboats that travelled between the island and its neighbours. The whole place looked like a Peter Stuyvesant advert. Any minute now I expected to see some beautiful people with perfect smiles and designer swimwear coming out of the water, sharing a pack of cigarettes and then driving off in a Ferrari. Everything was just too perfect to be true, but it was real. You could see why people wrote novels about the area and made James Bond movies here.

In the year 2000 Koh Phi Phi was still free of five star hotels and big businesses, but there were enough backpacker lodges, budget dive operators, restaurants and internet-cafés to make it perfect for our requirements. These requirements were simple: enough good Thai food, an ample supply of beer and the chance to meet interesting people with similar agendas to ours. The idyllic white beaches, world class dive sites and tropical location made Phi Phi very popular with travellers who wanted to zone out for a few weeks and then move on again. Some chose to stay for longer, like the guys who worked at the dive schools or the backpacker joints. Then there were those who simply lost the impetus to carry on travelling after a few too many spliffs in the hammock. It was a great place for us to wait for the ship's engine problems to be addressed more permanently and while Gavin, Ron and occasionally some others worked below deck, the rest of us had no alternative but to explore the island, dive the reefs and sample the best food we had tasted for quite a few months. The complete lack of surf in the area meant that we never got up early for dawn patrols and our nights became longer, sometimes stretching into the mornings. There were more full moon parties in the short time we spent there than there are full moons in a year and there were a number of discos and live bands.

The first thing that must have struck any visitor to the town would have been the celebration of the phallic form all over the place. Instead of garden gnomes, people here had model penises in various lurid colours in their front yards; they were in little parks where children played and in front of temples. They varied in size and shape; the largest one we saw was six feet high, complete with bulging veins and skin folds. I know that so-called lingams are found throughout the East and as far west as the Maldives, symbolizing fertility and masculinity, but the examples that I had previously seen were abstract poles that could pass for innocent fence posts. Here there was absolutely no chance for misinterpretation. I think these statues must have started out as genuine religious artefacts and that they were probably adapted for the benefit of tourists like me, while at the same time still being considered valid cultural objects by at least some of the local people. But it was somewhat unsettling to see little old ladies casually leaning against giant penises while chatting in the village square!

In an article I once read about (I think) Bali, the author said that the glory days of a town like Kuta happen just before the place goes to hell. (Clearly Kuta has been to hell and back a few times. Currently it's in some kind of Australian themed purgatory.) I think we saw Koh Phi Phi just in time. Shortly after our visit the developers moved in en mass and started building more hotels and resorts. Big budget feature films were being made in the vicinity and the playboys were arriving. Of course the 2004 tsunami then caused a lot of damage there and I wonder what the islands look like now.

When we were not enjoying the attractions in the village, we kept ourselves busy paddling around the tiny islands in our sea kayak and exploring the interior of Phi Phi on foot. The only person who did not seem to be enjoying the delights of the island much was Gavin. Ron remained his only confidant and most of the time he secluded himself in the engine room. It wasn't just a case of the rest of us gaily setting off on yet another lark in paradise every day, leaving our captain to do all the work. Gavin actively discouraged us from helping him. Ron and Francois were tolerated in the hot and claustrophobic innards of the ship, but mostly Gavin seemed to prefer tinkering there by himself, alone. The subject of Gavin's low mood and his ability to captain our ship became more and more prominent in our minds. Would we make it back safely through storms, uncharted reefs and countless unnamed islands with him at the helm? A growing sense of unease was becoming perceptible on board.

To take our minds off these worries, we kept ourselves busy. Some of the surrounding islets had been eroded away in the centre, forming enclosed lakes. At high tide a few of these communicated with the sea and one could paddle in through a tunnel in the cliffs. We glided along the smooth surface of one these lagoons in the kayak, surrounded by sheer rock faces towering high above us, cutting off the sun for most of the day. The surface of the water was like a mirror, completely undisturbed by wind or wave action. Paddling through it with the kayak was like unzipping a tightly stretched piece of material, revealing different colours underneath the top layer. The ripples produced by the craft fanned out behind us in a V-shape, exposing darker blues. We could see ferns growing in crevasses and hanging over the cliffs from the top, with bright flowers visible here and there. Birds flew overhead and sometimes they descended to the surface of the lagoon, but mostly it was almost eerily quiet inside these walls, as if we were inside a deserted citadel. There was talk of secret beaches hidden away amongst the overhangs and we searched for them, but without success. You could spend a lifetime discovering hidden places and treasures here.

Eventually I managed to convince Sean to come along on a walk through the overgrown interior of Koh Phi Phi. There was always something colourful or fragrant over the next rise, so it was late in the afternoon when we made it back to the ship. As we climbed on deck, we were surprised to see three beautiful girls. Francois, Richard and André had been entertaining them with beers and stories of the sea and everyone was having a great time. It transpired that they had met in one of the little restaurants ashore. While our boys were sipping coffee, these three beauties had come walking in. Now, this was not long after South Africans had started travelling again internationally after a long period of being prevented from doing so because of apartheid and the accompanying sanctions. Nowadays it is common to bump into other Safs abroad, but at the time it was highly unlikely, especially in Thailand. One can therefore forgive Francois and André for making fairly loud remarks about the girls to each other in Afrikaans, thinking that nobody else understood. They were discussing things such as scores out of ten for looks, likely bra sizes and sexual preference when the girls walked over to them and greeted them warmly in Afrikaans. They were from Pretoria, the heartland of Afrikaans speakers. I suppose it says something about the guys' charm that they managed to improve matters to the point where the girls agreed to join them on board the ship and that things were looking very merry indeed when Sean and I arrived.

The sun was starting to set and so we made plans for the evening. We agreed to rendezvous with the girls at a place called Patpong's later that evening. In the meantime we went for supper and a few beers later we arrived at a venue where a live band was playing. They were doing covers of all the old rock songs we liked, with a new take on the words. (Imagine Stairway to Heaven sang in falsetto Thai.) Apparently they were awful, but I remember enjoying the music incredibly and I was later told that I was asking everybody why we had never heard of this great band in the West. Several of us danced enthusiastically in front of the stage, making sure we didn't become dehydrated in the hot night air by drinking more beer. Later we were invited (I think) onto the stage by the lead singer, who clearly enjoyed our appreciation of his music and we spent quite a while there, until some people from the audience kindly helped us down to the dance floor so that the singer could get to the mike again. We decided to chill out a little and got more beer. The rest of the evening passed in a blur and I can only remember fragments. At some stage I noticed that Sean's face had turned into wax, like the models at Madame Tussaud's and that it was melting in the heat and running down towards his chin. He looked like one of those Salvador Dali clocks, just quite red; but in spite of his appearance he seemed to be in very good spirits and full of energy. Eventually we did make it to Patpongs and we met up with the girls from Pretoria, but for some reason they were irritated with us and they didn't want to dance. That's a pity, because we absolutely killed it on the dance floor, giving a fine demonstration of African rhythm. People were so impressed that the floor quickly cleared and everyone was watching us. Only a few of them left, unfortunately including the Afrikaans girls.

The last nightspot had finally closed its doors and it was time to get back to the Explorer for some well-deserved rest. When we arrived on the beach, the tide had receded so far that it was impossible to drag our tender down to the waterline. We had to spend the remainder of the night on the sand with the mosquitoes until the tide came in again. The garlic in the curry we had eaten or possibly the amount of booze in our systems must have deterred the mozzies, because we woke up at sunrise with only a few bites. With team effort we managed to launch the boat and we made our way back to the ship without any mishaps. Only Francois fell in the water when we climbed onto the Explorer from the tender.

When we woke up later and went ashore for our breakfast, we were greeted warmly by several complete strangers, received high fives in the street and we heard a good deal of laughter around us. At least most people seemed pleased to see us, even though we suspected they were laughing at us, not with us. We decided that this was a sure sign that the time had come to move on and so we finished our banana shakes and our coffees, cleared out the local pharmacy's supply of aspirin and went to discuss our itinerary with Gavin. He was rapidly losing his tan down in the engine room, but at least he was making progress with the repairs.

The news wasn't good. Gavin did not think that it would be wise to sail further on into the Andaman Sea. The ship's engine was not strong enough to withstand too many big storms and the isolated Andaman Islands and large tracts of open ocean were not the place to play pirates. If we did have mechanical failure, or ran aground, or even sank the ship, there would be even less chance of assistance than in the Mentawai

Islands, where one might be able to ask for help on the radio. In comparison with the potential in the Mentawais, the prospects of finding surf in the Andaman's were small. Much less swell filtered through to this part of the ocean than further south. Many of the crew were keen to head back to the known breaks of Sumatra. Jonno for instance had never been very keen to leave the quality surf of the Mentawais in the first place. He didn't care where he surfed; as long as he got good waves, he was happy. I think he would have been just as happy surfing hollow, powerful waves in a crowded, industrial neighbourhood as he would have been in the pristine picture perfect places that I dreamt about. For him it was all about the waves; for me it was the travelling and the adventure. The waves were the goal, but I suppose that for me, sometimes they are just an excuse to seek out new places.

In any event, the decision had been made to turn around, and once again I felt gutted. My dreams of having a really hardcore National Geographic experience in a totally wild place had finally been completely extinguished. And just think of the waves that find their way to those pristine shores every now and then. Very few people have ever seen these breaks and even fewer have surfed there. If I could have snagged just one, just a small wave in that area …

Who knows what would have happened to us if we had continued northwards. No doubt I would have been seasick for many days and there would have been many hours of fruitless searching for islands and reefs with surfable waves. Our diet would have been reduced to what we could catch, with very little fruit or vegetables. And when you go through a prolonged period of being cooped up together like this, tempers become short and arguments start. Things can become unpleasant quickly, especially with our cantankerous captain. But that's the nature of travelling and exploration.

We took the safe, sensible option, headed south and tried not to think of what could have been.

Chapter 4
Making the Grade

"One afternoon a few of us were on the beach, tossing a Frisbee around, when someone asked what the time was. Francois squinted into the sun, thought for a while and as he carelessly flicked the Frisbee back he replied, 'July ...'"

The Island Explorer left the clear, shallow water of Thailand and headed southwest for Sumatra. After a fairly uneventful crossing of the Straits of Malacca, we slowed down to look at some of the islands we had passed during the unfavourable weather on our way north. There were so many tiny islets that we just skimmed the surface of what was there, but eventually we were stopped by what looked like a classic set-up. White lines were running along a reef in front of some cliffs, symmetrically and mechanically, every wave seemingly identical to the one before it. Gavin steered the ship as close to the reef as was possible and four of us jumped into the water and paddled over to the break. The prospect of finding another G-land or Uluwatu made me hyperventilate as all four of us churned up the warm water to get to the spot first. I loved the feeling of being back on my surfboard again after the few weeks of enforced rest and the water felt like velvet on my skin. As we neared the waves, we could see them run along the reef and now that we were close, we noticed that they were zipping along much faster than they had appeared to be doing from further away. Francois caught the first one, but he did not make it past the initial section. I stroked into a clean looking wall, but as soon as I got to my feet, the wave ran away from me and I was left in the white wash. Ditto the rest of the guys. After a few more fruitless attempts to ride the waves, we had to concede defeat. These waves were perfect, but just too fast for us. We just could not ride these walls. Maybe an exceptional surfer would be able to negotiate the speeding barrels or possibly a different tide would help. For us it was game over and we had a long paddle back to the ship, some good old anchor pulling to do and then a prolonged wait until we reached the next possible break. We looked at other similar reefs, but found nothing surfable that day. After one or two repetitions of our first episode, we were tired and wary when we spotted another potential surf spot. The reality of surf exploration sank in quickly: like anything worthwhile, it is hard work and time consuming.

The next day, in a last ditch attempt to find waves in the area, we headed for a rocky outcrop further out to sea that was completely exposed to the Indian Ocean. There were no reefs or islands to block the swells from any direction. The Explorer approached the little islet from the north and we saw white water splashing high into the air along the rock's edges. To see whether the waves that were breaking here were surfable, Gavin edged the ship closer slowly. We had lowered and then hoisted the tender and the anchor enough times to make us loath to repeat that tedious and time consuming process again, so nobody complained when Gavin simply motored right up to the waves for a good look instead of launching the little boat. A new swell was running, still on the increase and every now and then a big set unloaded on the reef adjacent to the bare rocks that jutted out of the water. Gavin cut the engine and the ship drifted slowly. The waves that we looked at were big. Sets hit an outside reef and ran for a short distance before reaching a shallow inside shelf that made them jack up and bowl. This would be the dangerous part of the ride and we were wondering whether it was worth risking it. After such a long time without surfing, we were all keen to have a go, but we were apprehensive of these waves. They were full of raw energy and power.

After a spell of studying the waves, Francois glanced at our position in the water and said, "Gavin, we're getting a little close to those rocks, hey."

"Don't worry, I've got her." But Gavin did not adjust course or switch on the engine. We continued to drift closer to the impact zone. Now the rest of us were starting to feel uneasy as well, but Gavin kept staring ahead at the waves.

"Don't you think we're getting a little close, Gavin?" Richard now spoke up.

"We're fine, we're fine." He kept staring at the waves, not really looking at the surrounding sea. The ship was now rocking markedly with every set that came by.

"Time to steer away now, Gav. We're too close!" Francois' voice had some urgency to it.

"Oh, keep your pants on!" Gavin reached over to switch the engine on with an irritated look on his face. He pressed the ignition switch, but for some unknown reason nothing happened. He glanced up nervously, scanning the sea ahead of us and then his expression changed. A big set was building on the outside reef, bigger than any of the previous ones. He pressed the switch again and thankfully this time the engine turned over and rumbled to life. But we had drifted too far in. The Explorer was now lying almost parallel to the approaching waves, in danger of getting a broadside hit which could capsize her. The only way to get out of the situation was to motor even closer to the reef in order to turn perpendicular to the waves and then to steer over them. The swells were now starting to feather on the outside, spray blowing backwards off their crests, and they were advancing strait towards us. I grabbed hold of the wooden counter in front of me in the wheelhouse as we slowly came around to face the oncoming waves. So far we were still clear of the reef, that much we could be glad of. But the whole set of rumbling waves were now bearing down on us and all I could focus on was line upon line of blue-black water towering into the sky. Gavin was murmuring to himself, "Oh shit, oh shit, oh shit!" louder and louder, as if he were praying to some scatological god that refused to hear. I wished for a seatbelt, but I was very relieved that at least I was inside the wheelhouse and not on the front deck, where Johnno, Es, André and Derek were now desperately clinging to whatever they could find to hang on to. We went over the first wave relatively easily, lurching first up, then down into the trough. Gavin pushed the throttle open and we powered through the second wave as well, but two more waves, much bigger than the previous ones, were now coming at us. I could see the people on the deck screaming, their faces contorted with a mixture of fear and determination, wet with sea spray, their eyes wide. But I could hear nothing over the roar of the engine and the thundering ocean. It was like watching a silent movie in slow motion. A silent horror movie.

As we went up the face of the third wave, it felt as if we were going to fall over backwards, so steep was the angle of the ship, but the Explorer broke through the lip of the wave, crashing down, her bowsprit digging into the trough as water streamed over the deck, running down hatches and washing buckets, clothes and whatever was left lying around on deck into the sea. The bow of the ship popped up into the air again and the ship rolled from side to side, like a wet dog shaking off water, then she righted herself. Like a weary boxer getting up after being knocked down in the ring, the Explorer faced her nemesis once again. She moved forward sluggishly and unsteadily, wobbling towards the last wave of the set as it reared up. We had to make it over this wave before it broke; those on deck might not be able to hold on again and I wasn't sure whether the ship would stay upright either. The engine was already going at maximum power and there was nothing to do but hope and pray that we would reach the crest before it smashed into us. Once again the bow started to climb into the air. Up, up, up we went, the water boiling alongside the ship, the entire vessel straining. Then suddenly we were over it, plunging down behind the breaker just as the lip flailed forward and walloped the reef. We had made it! By a hair's breadth, but we made it. Gavin slowly eased off on the throttle, then opened his water bottle with a quick twist and drained its entire contents in one long gulp. As we headed out to the safety of deeper water, those on deck struggled to their feet, dazed and bewildered. Melissa and Ron emerged from below, battered and bruised from being tossed out of their bunks. We all stared around, too stunned to talk, too shocked to even whimper. We just stared.

Nobody said anything to Gavin. What was there to say? He had made a big mistake that almost had dire consequences. We all knew it and he knew it better than anyone else. The ship slowly motored back to the more protected islands.

From that point on Gavin became even more reclusive than he had previously been. For long periods he spoke to almost nobody. He started spending entire days in his cabin, leaving the running of the ship to Francois and Richard. By now everybody aboard was very familiar with the ship's daily routine, so as long as the weather remained good and the engine held out, we managed well. But obviously we were worried about the situation.

We spent another day in the area and then we moved on. The islands had perfect, but useless waves. Here one would have been able to take the kind of photos we see in magazines so often: empty line-ups, sunny skies and perfect barrels in an impressive setting. But the illusion dissolved in the transparent water when it came to riding the waves. The other problem was that it was often difficult to find a safe anchorage just before dusk in these unknown parts. We started dreading the nights. Just as we fell asleep, the wind would change and the call would come to pull up the anchor. We'd all have to line up on deck, heave on the rope and then the ship would have to motor to another position. After all the commotion it was difficult to fall asleep again. People became ratty and tempers grew short.

On the days when Gavin did skipper the ship, he would sometimes spot a protected bay in the afternoon and decide to stay for the night. Then there would be discontent aboard the Explorer. We'd protest about the waste of daylight time. What about that next bay where the perfect wave might be hiding? But as captain, Gavin was responsible for our safety as well as that of the ship and he always had the last word. After our close call he was now over-cautious, taking no more chances. As time wore on, we avoided arguments with the taciturn Cornishman. He was starting to look increasingly strained and harassed. Sometimes there was a different look about him, something far-off, almost baleful. The responsibility of captaining the ship was clearly too much for him.

Then one day he started to collect rain water. The Explorer had two large tanks below deck, which we had filled before we left Lankawi. It should have been enough for several weeks' consumption at least, but Gavin became obsessed with making sure that we would not die of thirst. He insisted that we collect water whenever it rained and instructed us to put buckets, water bottles and pots under the run-off from the roof of the wheelhouse and the tarpaulin that we used for shade. All of this was carefully stored.

We had been showering and washing our clothes in sea water right from the outset of our voyage. The fresh water supply was too small to allow any use except for drinking and cooking. So we were well aware that our water was scarce and we were all careful not to waste this resource, but now Gavin really started to become fixated by liquid.

And then one night he really over-stepped the mark. I was woken up by Es' angry voice.

"Are you crazy? What time is it? It's the middle of the night, that's whatta time it is! Me, collect water now just because it's raining? Have-a you lost your mind, Gaveen? I'm going back to sleep now. Good night!"

I suppose a lot of us were lying in our bunks half asleep, asking ourselves the same question that Es had asked Gavin: Has our captain now finally gone crazy? Has he gone around the bend? Had we pushed him too far? Did he sail beyond the edges of safety and sanity like Captain Kurtz in Apocalypse Now, who had ventured so far into the tropics that he reached a place where he could no longer distinguish right from wrong? Was the engine room Gavin's equivalent of Kurtz's dark lair of madness? Did he keep a stowaway hidden there to keep him company? Yes, of course! That is why he needs so much water! Maybe he has a few people there, a concubine or two ...

In the morning the light of day straightened out my thoughts somewhat, but I still wondered about Gavin. I wondered whether he was anticipating that we would be marooned on a remote island or drift helplessly at sea if our engine failed. Or maybe he knew something about the seaworthiness of the ship that the rest of us did not. However, the recurring thought in my mind was always, did we really want to be at the mercy of some unstable Limey in the middle of nowhere? Was it time to relieve him of his captaincy?

Derek and I conferred about Gavin's deteriorating state of mind and we agreed to talk to him discreetly when an opportunity presented itself.

"Listen, there's nothing wrong with me!" Gavin was not happy about my enquiries. "You'd be just as stressed if you were in charge of this jumble of planks that you call a ship. And I have to rely on you lot of land lubbers who have never set foot on a boat before to help me sail it. You know nothing, man! And water is precious. You only have to go without it once to realise that it's not worth taking chances over."

Derek's overtures were met with a similar rebuff, so we decided to leave Gavin alone for a while.

At least the diving was good amongst these islands and we found undisturbed marine life everywhere we looked. Nowhere did we see another soul. This tiny archipelago was just too remote and isolated to live in permanently. We continued onwards through the unknown, looking for inhabited islands.

It was around this time that I caught my big fish. When we were travelling slowly, we always had a lure or two dragging in the water behind the ship. Sometimes a fish would grab the bait and when there was no time to go spear fishing this could provide a welcome meal. I was sitting at the table in the stern of the ship with my eyes on the horizon and my thoughts somewhere in the clouds when the shrill sound of a spinning reel jerked me to my feet. I hadn't done any fishing since I'd given it up as a teenager, but it had been quite a few days since we had eaten anything but dreary rations from the ship's stores and the thought of another plate of noodles with tinned tomato paste made me grab the fishing rod with an urgency that surprised me. Pulling in a fish is like riding a bicycle: once you've acquired the skill your body remembers what to do without thinking. The instant I held the rod I knew that I had a big one on the hook. I was instinctively playing out the line, and then reeling it in when there was some slack, heaving on the rod and feeling it vibrate as if it was part of me. It wasn't an even contest, because the fish had to fight the rod as well as swim against the power of our engine. But that was just hard luck for the fish. We were hungry and we were prepared to get our food by any means. But that did not mean that our quarry was going to give in without trying everything it could. It dived down deeply and tried to swim under the ship. It even tried to jump to freedom, but it was doomed. It struggled until it had no strength left, then the silver body broke through the surface of the water for the last time, the gaff went in and we had it on board, thrashing around – a beautiful Dorado, full of colour. Everything became a blur of water, scales, blood and teeth and then the knife found its mark and everything was over. The fish lay on deck, suddenly still, its colour ebbing away slowly, blood spreading out from its gills where we had thrust in the knife. I was filled with pride, exhilaration, sadness, loss and regret. Are those the ingredients of guilt?

On the horizon we saw a thin trail of smoke going straight up into the still air. We steered the ship towards it, hoping for a village where we could buy some fruit and vegetables. We were down to our last papaya and every morning we scraped the hairy fungus from its surface and sliced a few pieces for breakfast, mixing it with banana slices and limejuice to hide the overripe taste. I was hoping for some green coconuts as well. They lasted long and I found the coconut milk more refreshing than warm beer. The onboard freezer was just managing to keep things slightly cool and the fridge was only good to keep flies away from our food.

This little village was on the sheltered side of the island and there was a good place to anchor close to the houses. As usual we launched the tender to look for surf and we motored around the island to the exposed part. Here we found a nice right-hander breaking in front of a stand of coconut palms. A breeze came up and started blowing cross-shore, making the surface choppy, but this was a bona fide surfable wave and we all jumped in and caught a few before dusk. The conditions weren't great, but it felt good to surf again after a long lay-off. Thinking back on it now, it was good for my surfing to have had a break. I had learned a lot of new things and it was as if my sub-conscious needed the time to process all of this and make sense of it. Now I felt more comfortable and confident in the surf.

Everyone was awake at first light the next morning. Jonno and Es went ashore with their video camera and hiked across the island to the surf spot, while Melissa and Richard went shopping in the village. The rest of us headed straight for the waves. This time there was no wind and the breakers ran smoothly along the reef. We took turns riding the head high waves, stretching our muscles and enjoying the sensation of feeling our surfboards under our feet again. After a while one of us remarked that something felt different here. The dynamic in the water had changed; the pace was slower and more relaxed. Then it dawned on us that this was the first place we were surfing without Gerhard. He always competed hard for the set waves, harassing whoever might be on the inside and now he wasn't there to egg us on and to push us into deeper take-offs; to make us paddle back faster. Gerhard had left and so we named this right-hander Gerhard's Left. It's corny, but the name stuck. I wonder whether Gerhard ever heard about this dubious honour that befell him.

As the tide became lower, a section of the wave started to barrel. It wasn't Nias or HT's, but it was a barrel for sure. I took off on a medium sized wave and built up some speed, watching the section ahead of me suck out. I came into the section fairly high on the wave face, ducked my head under the cascading lip and all of a sudden there I was, inside the tube, that place we all try to reach when we surf, so elusive and so utterly indescribable. My eyes were on the opening ahead of me, my ears filled with the roar of the sea. At the fringes of my vision I saw white foam move up the face and over with the lip in front of me. I saw little pieces of seaweed go by and I glimpsed Derek paddling over the shoulder of the wave, far off. I willed my body forward through the narrow tunnel, just managing to avoid the wall of water that arched over my head and exploded around me. My momentum carried me through into the sunshine and I emerged a new man. At last I had negotiated a real tube here in Indonesia. Finally I had managed to ride through a section of the wave fully behind the curtain, cut off from the outside world for a second or two. I flew onto the open face, kicked out over the back of the wave and fell back into the water laughing. What a feeling! I was relieved, elated, proud and energised - stoked!

After that morning's session I re-lived that barrel-ride many times, feeling the goose pimples, hearing the sounds and seeing the spray in my mind's eye. I later read a piece Kelly Slater wrote about barrel-riding and what immediately struck me was that he said he never remembers hearing anything when he is inside the tube. For me the most memorable aspect of being inside is that rushing, roaring sound. It mesmerises me and most of the time it impresses me so much, I fall off my board. I suppose that's one of the differences between a champ and a kook. He takes in only what is necessary to negotiate the barrel whereas I become completely overwhelmed by the experience. But actually I don't mind my lack of focus so much. Kelly is missing out on some of the best sounds in the universe. And listening to a recording of that sound will be worthless. You have to feel it with your body.

As with many other things in life, once I had managed that first proper tube ride, just knowing that I could do it made things a lot easier. I got another barrel that morning before the wind came up and ended the session. On my way back to the ship I reviewed my progress as a surfer during our voyage. I was now at a point where I did not find it painful to be honest with myself about my abilities in the water. After many weeks in Sumatra I had finally managed what most surfers have to do within the space of a ten day surf charter if they want to be able to say that they got value for their money: get barrelled. Let's face it, if you come all the way here and you don't get shacked off your nut, it's been a waste. I realised that I was a long way off getting the kind of tubes you see in video footage of this area, but at the same time, if I compared my surfing during my first sessions in the Mentawais to now, I was happy. Now that I had managed some barrels, I was optimistic about getting more, but I knew that Gerhard's left was a relatively easy wave. Scoring tubes in the powerful and more crowded setups further south would be more difficult. And backhand tube rides were another kettle of fish entirely. Surfing with one's back to the wave makes positioning in the tube more difficult, especially when the waves are fast and the reef shallow. I still had a long way to go before I would be able to say that I had done the waves of the Mentawais justice. To do that I would need to ride more tubes and I would have to get a good few seconds behind the lip on a decent backhander. I resolved to push myself until I managed to do that.

Later in the day when we spoke to Jonno and Es, they said that we weren't the first to surf at this island. The villagers had asked them about Bob, an Australian who had arrived on a fishing boat a year or two earlier with a sack of rice, a surfboard and very little else. They assumed that we would know him because we also surfed. These islanders had very little contact with the outside world and they had no idea of how big it all is. They reminded me of those Americans (the ones with the loud shirts and even louder voices) who ask you whether you know Mike in Kenya when they hear you're from South Africa. But Americans have access to education, multi media and the money to enlighten themselves about the world. Bob stayed in the village, surfed the waves for a month and then left for an unknown destination when his rice ran out. That is hardcore surf travel. In comparison we had it so easy with our mobile shelter, storage for food and a (relatively) reliable way to move between locations.

I was keen to have another session at Gerhard's Left and later that afternoon Ron dropped a few of us off at the surf spot. After an hour or so the tender came around to pick us up, but there was always another good wave on the horizon and Derek, Sean and I decided to stay on and to find our way back to the ship on our own steam later. As the sun started dipping towards the horizon, we picked our way across the reef and jogged along the shore to a point close to where the Explorer was anchored. It was dark when we started paddling out across the little bay towards the ship. We were aware of sharks of course and their feeding habits around dusk, so we dipped our arms into the inky water gingerly, making short, superficial strokes. At one stage I struck a floating coconut and I nearly ran the rest of the way to the ship from fright. The darker the sky became, the jumpier we got and the longer the distance between the ship and the three of us seemed to stretch. It took forever to get to the ship, but eventually we all made it with our limbs still attached and that coconut was the closest I ever came to a shark attack in Indonesia. The next morning we pulled up the anchor and set the course for Lagundri again. What we did not know was that we had some very nasty stowaways aboard the ship.

Francois was the first guy who became painfully aware that everything was not all right on board. He woke up on our first morning away from land with four or five very red and swollen welts on his body. We weren't sure what was causing them. Could he be allergic to some food, was he being bitten by an insect, or did he have a mysterious tropical illness? Then Melissa got the same painful marks and shortly afterwards Richard succumbed to the mystery affliction. They had headaches, felt nauseous and the welts started to fester in the tropical heat, necessitating antibiotic treatment to prevent the sores from developing into tropical ulcers. Now the conspiracy theories started and as usual, Es was first: "I tell you now, it's Gaveen! He is going to poison us all. Just last night I saw him in the galley pretending to make coffee. When he saw me, he walked away. I swear he was trying to put something in the sugar. And who takes the most sugar in his coffee? Francois! Who never takes any sugar? Gaveen!" She looked at us triumphantly.

"I'm not so sure, Es," Johnno cautioned her. "Ya never actually saw him put anything in the sugar did ya? So don't jump to conclusions, silly Sheila. I saw him walking around with that can of insecticide near the cooking pot last night and, let's face it, the food tasted pretty rank, didn't it? And I'm just recalling it now, but he chucked his food over board last night and took a few Beng-Bengs later."

"Do you really think he's spraying poison in our food?"

"Yeah, that's why my arse burned so much last time I crapped!"

It was only after a few days that we found the first culprit in somebody's bunk. The sleeping person had crushed a small black scorpion.

And then we found lots of them. They were in the woodwork of our cabins, in the galley cupboards and sometimes they fell onto us from somewhere overhead. We were being attacked by a malevolent force of tiny automatons and we were never sure where they would spring from next. It was impossible to relax and I felt like going to bed with a can of insecticide under my pillow. (Even though scorpions are not insects we soon discovered that they were kind enough to succumb quite quickly to a squirt of Doom.) Eventually we discovered how they had come on board. A large bunch of bananas was hanging from the roof of the galley and here the mother scorpion sat, still nursing a number of offspring on her back. Of course, we had to exterminate the lot, but it took a long time to find them all and for a week or two we were still checking our bunks very carefully before retiring. It wasn't uncommon to be woken up in the middle of the night by a shout, a few choice swear words and then some hard stomping around in the dark. Luckily I was never stung by one of these critters.

Es wasn't happy with this turn of events. "Well, yes, I did buy that bunch of bananas, but it definitely had not even one scorpio on it! He put them on the bunch afterwards, I saw him hanging around them often."

After a quick stop at Nias, we headed for the islands of Asu and Bawa. A surfing contest was under way in Lagundri and the contestants were in the water most of the time, preparing for their heats. The waves were relatively small and it would be difficult to get any good rides under these circumstances. Of course neither us, nor the villagers of Lagundri had forgotten the unpleasant incidents during our previous visit, so we did not spend the night there.

After drifting around the paradisiacal islands of South East Asia for so many weeks, I had become so used to our beautiful surroundings that I had to remind myself how fortunate I was to be there. When I think back on it now, the searing white beaches and translucent water covering technicolor reefs seem like a fantasy, something that I had dreamed up, but at that time I almost didn't notice the beauty any more. I had to say to myself, "Look at these incredible bays filled with so much beauty!" The emerald jungle spilled from the interior of the islands onto the sand, only kept in check by the spring tides that periodically washed up to its edges. We would scan the shorelines for signs of life and every so often a bush pig with gleaming tusks or perhaps a brightly coloured jungle fowl would emerge from the thicket, run along the shore for a brief spell and then disappear from view again.

Johnno would look at them longingly. "Don't ya think we could shoot one of those porkers with a spear gun mate? I can already smell the chops on the barbie ... "

"Oh Johnno, can't you just appreciate what we have here in front of us without thinking of your stomach?" Melissa would say this with mock indignation, but with a yearning expression in her eyes. We were all starting to think with our stomachs.

Bawa was fun in the smallish surf, but towards the evening, the swell started to pick up and we headed to Asu in anticipation of bigger waves the next day. We anchored in the lee of the island just as the sun sank below the horizon.

Back home in more temperate climes, watching the sunset is a long, leisurely affair. People have drinks while lounging around, glancing at the horizon now and then and they continue their unhurried conversations while the sun slowly goes to sleep.

In the tropics there is no drawn out nightfall. The whole affair is over in a few short minutes and if you want to take a picture, you better have your camera ready. But the colours are intense and the foreground is never dull. No matter how many travel brochures I look at or how many holiday pics I see, tropical sunsets continue to captivate me. When the sun is in just the right place, the golden glint on the leaves of the palm trees transforms the skyline from a mere hint of what lies beyond to a brilliant facade for just a few moments. My imagination magnifies that picture into a wonderland. And then that fleeting glimpse is gone but for the memory of it in my mind.

When I was a child, I had a story book about a mouse called Frederick, who collected colours. While his peers frantically foraged for food to store for the cold winter months, Frederick drank in pictures, sensations and experiences. He had no supplies of nuts or acorns like the other mice and they scolded him about it. But in the dead of winter when it was dark for weeks on end, he delved into his memories and the colours and the stories that he shared with the other mice kept them all happy and warm in a way that food could not. I have stored the colours from those sunsets in my mind for the same purpose.

Throughout the next day the swell increased in size and the head high waves we surfed in the morning had doubled in size by lunch time. I was tired and still wary of this wave after my humbling experience on our previous visit, so after a day of good waves I was happy to watch the surf from the ship with a Bintang in my hand. Gavin had spent most of the day in the engine room again and he emerged from below deck in a foul mood. He was in the wrong frame of mind when he jumped overboard with his surfboard and stroked out towards the surf.

Gavin later told me that he really wanted to smash the waves to get rid of his frustration. He didn't care that the swell had increased even more since the early afternoon; he was a big guy. He was angry and Asu was going to feel it.

But you don't mess with the sea. It took only one wave to set things straight between Gavin and Mother Ocean.

"I was still paddling for that wave when the whole thing

just jacked up and threw me down," Gavin told me a few days later. "I went down so quickly, I didn't even know I was under water. Then it whacked my head into my board so hard I nearly passed out, but I knew I had to stay conscious, otherwise I'd drown. I couldn't do anything, the wave was too powerful, and so I just concentrated on holding my breath."

He paused to breathe deeply and then he carried on talking.

"That wave just wouldn't let up and I was out of air, plus the knock on the noggin had really concussed me. I kept expecting that I would faint and drown any second.

"You know I don't believe in an afterlife. When you die, you cease to exist, like a light switch has been flipped off. So while I could still feel the wave suffocating me, I knew that I was alive. That was kinda good, if you know what I mean. It actually surprised me that I still cared about being alive. I always thought that death would be a relief, but down there in the darkness I realised that I still wanted to live. So I started to swim for the surface. I popped out of the water like a cork and I remember just sucking air. Ahh, it felt so good, so sweet!"

He touched his eye reflexively.

"But then I noticed I was blind in my right eye and that scared the shit out of me. I couldn't see where I was and the waves kept on battering me. There was blood in the water everywhere around me and I knew I was in deep trouble. I don't know how long this carried on for, but I just went into a kind of stupor. Then I felt Ron lifting me onto a board and he started pushing me out of the impact zone. I remember saying to him, 'I'm blind, I'm blind,' but he just kept on telling me that it's ok over and over again, like he didn't believe it. That's when I knew that I was in pretty bad shape. It took forever to get to the ship, like in a nightmare. I don't know how they got me up the ladder and onto the deck, the next I remember was your face looking down at me, like I was the Antichrist." He chuckled.

"Well, you looked like something from a horror movie," I

said. "Like someone had attacked you with an axe! I thought you were really seriously injured, probably a brain injury or something. It's been a long time since I felt that scared. You know what a nightmare it would be to get someone to a hospital from here; it's almost impossible. By the time we would have managed to get you to a proper facility, you would have been dead if it was serious."

I remember feeling ice cold as I watched Ron and Francois carry Gavin towards me where I was waiting for them in the stern. Blood was streaming from Gavin's head and I knew that we had no equipment or facilities to deal with a serious head injury. If there was bleeding inside the skull, Gavin could die within hours. Derek was out surfing, blissfully unaware of what was happening. It was my responsibility to deal with Gavin and I felt very alone. As we laid him down on the table where we usually played cards, I was praying to any and all of the gods available that Gavin had been dealt a good hand. His face was streaming with blood and his scalp was hanging down over his face like a curtain, obscuring his right eye and revealing patches of white skull on his forehead. Gavin had been scalped by his own surfboard. He had knocked two of the fins that were glassed onto his big wave board clean off with his head. That takes some doing. I knew that the force required to do this kind of damage was enough to cause serious brain injuries.

"What a relief it was when you lifted that piece of skin that covered my eye and I could see out of it again!"

"Ja, I was just as glad. It was amazing how few serious injuries you actually had, given the way you looked. I was just waiting to find that you were paralysed or you didn't have sensation somewhere, but everything seemed fine. Of course I was still worried that there could be some bleeding inside your skull or some other problems that would only become apparent later, but I didn't say anything."

"Yeah, you just kept on telling me how lucky I am and I was thinking, 'If that's what you call lucky I don't want to see the unlucky bastards you've treated!'"

"And then we had that marathon suturing session. It took at least an hour to put you back together again. All by torchlight! But look at you now; I think I actually might have improved your looks somewhat!"

Actually, Gavin resembled a resurrected evil mummy. I had put in countless sutures to get the scalp back into place. It looked like someone had attempted a brain transplant on him. For the next few days Gavin wandered about the ship with a haphazardly shaved head, a massively swollen blue eye and bandages twisted about his face. Frankenstein's monster would have been scared of him. It's a pity we had no pirates or unwanted officials on board. We had the perfect deterrent for them!

As the time passed and it became apparent that Gavin had not been too badly damaged, Derek and I relaxed again and we started to settle into the laid back pattern of passing time on Asu. The swell had moved on again and normally we would have sailed for the next group of islands, but we decided to stay a while in order for Gavin to recuperate. To pass the time we lounged under the palms, snorkelled the reefs and drank the beer at Vincent's. We had long since lost track of time. One afternoon a few of us were on the beach, tossing a Frisbee around, when someone asked what the time was. Francois squinted into the sun, thought for a while and as he carelessly flicked the Frisbee back he replied, "July ..."

His laconic answer summed up our priorities pretty well. We knew that there were many people in grey suits around the world who were desperately watching the clock, working against deadlines and worrying about time and money, but it was a different world from ours. Where we were, money could buy you a beer or two, but little else. The ocean encompassed our world and waves were our currency. We avoided talking about work and of going back to our previous lives. The subject would have been distasteful; we just weren't interested in the kind of places where things like shoes, underwear and shampoo were considered necessary. But we all knew that our eventual return to the real world was unavoidable. In the meantime, we drank a toast there on the beach, to all those people to whom it mattered that it was Monday.

A soldier with a gun poked his head into my cabin and peered at me. I sat up, still sleepy and nauseous from my usual affliction and stared back. He stepped inside and looked in my bags, glanced around the cabin and left again. I followed him.

In the wheelhouse Gavin, Richard and Francois were negotiating with a senior-looking officer with lots of epaulettes, badges and emblems on his jacket. He was paging through the ship's registration documents with a scowl on his face. A patrol boat had flagged us down and a routine inspection of the ship was under way. After Gavin had recovered enough from his head injury, we had been sailing south, back to the well-known surf spots and as we came closer to Padang, we started seeing other charter yachts and now also the Indonesian Coast Guard. From my admittedly limited experience with them, military men all over the world seem to love only one thing more than shooting guns and that is finding fault with paper work. Nothing untoward had been found on board, as all the discounted cigarettes and other combustible herbs had been consumed during the preceding weeks at sea and Indie the parakeet had flown away. No doubt we would have been charged with importing illegal merchandise and wildlife if we still had those. (What I did not know at the time was that a certain crewmember had left a rather explicit "glamour" DVD in a bag under my bunk. I discovered it there a few weeks later and only then did its owner remember about it. He explained that it had been added to a purchase he had made in Medan to sweeten the deal. We refrained from asking what he had been buying in the first place. Fortunately the soldier who had inspected my cabin did not look under my bunk. It could have been rather embarrassing to say the least.) Anyway, whether there was anything illegal on board was largely irrelevant. The soldiers were in a position of power and they were going to use it to extract some cash from us. It was only a question of how much. To make the matter seem as serious as possible, the commanding officer dragged out the inspection of papers for as long as he could. After that, the discussion about the documents took forever. Certain irregularities were pointed out and we were informed that the ship was operating entirely illegally. Lengthy negotiations followed and a fine was finally agreed upon. We wished that we could just have paid this amount to the soldiers right when they boarded us, to cut the whole unsavoury affair short, but of course the officer had to save face. We could do nothing but sit and wait for him to finish his charade, pay up and greet the search party with a few descriptive Afrikaans swear words as they left.

As soon as the soldiers were out of sight, we motored to the nearest break to wash off the feeling of being abused. Telescopes is another popular spot and we arrived to see two other boats anchored at the break. There were a number of professional surfers on the waves, with a cameraman in the water and another one in a little inflatable boat hovering near the line-up. They were busy filming a surf movie and they looked busy. Some other travelling surfers were also trying to catch a few of the clean left-handers that came through. After watching the performance for a while, some of us paddled toward the break. The vibe in the water was tense, the pros looking angry and frustrated and the feeling seemed to have rubbed off on the other surfers. A well-known surfer from Hawaii, known for his not-so-sunny disposition, was cursing at no one in particular, complaining about the waves, the sunburn, the humidity and all the kooks in the water. I watched him getting longer barrels than anybody else, but his mood did not change. He complained about the crummy little boat they were cooped up in, the lousy food and the aircon in his cabin that wasn't cool enough. He could not phone home and he didn't know what the latest NFL standings were. This was just another shitty job for him and all he wanted was to finish this damned photo shoot and get back home. There was no etiquette in the water. The pros paddled past everyone else, snaked each other and dropped in on us. I headed back to the Explorer without catching a wave. It would have been preferable to surf one-foot onshore junk to those ideally shaped walls.

J. M. Barry once said that nothing is really work, except if you'd rather be doing something else. Perfect tropical reefs were nothing new to these jaded surfers and they would rather have been doing something else. Being in paradise was a chore to them and surfing had become just another dreary occupation. They had lost the stoke.

I tried to picture how wonderful this place must have seemed to the first few surfers who had come to these shores in the time before the crowds and the charter industry. It must have been idyllic, but now the fantasy had been destroyed. And some of the very people who were showcasing the beautiful waves of the islands to the surfing world were the most negative and cynical of all. What a contrast to what it must have seemed like to the original surfers who came here. Of course I was also one of those contributing to the changes that were transforming the islands. I had followed other people to these shores and now I too was paddling for the inside, trying to catch a wave and in the process crowding the Mentawais a little more. Just a few years after it had been discovered, this surfing nirvana was already on its way to hell. In my mind's eye I could already see the tacky tourist stalls on the beaches and the cheesy postcards, together with the T-shirts that say, "My boyfriend went to the Mentawais and all he brought me was this lousy shirt."

Looking back on it now, more than a decade later, things have not turned out quite as badly as I had thought they might, but a wave to yourself in the Mentawais in season would be a rare thing these days. Most of the well-known spots now have surf camps, guaranteeing a crowd every day when there are waves. When conditions are unfavourable at other spots, speedboats bring residents from other camps to add to the number of people trying to catch a wave. Of course, there are many charter boats in the islands and now that information about the required winds, tides and swell for each reef is common knowledge, it would be impossible to slip away to a hidden corner for a quiet surf session. We didn't realise it at the time, but we were very fortunate to have been able to surf quite a few of the spots without having anybody else in the vicinity.

As I sat on board, contemplating the demise of carefree surfing in the Mentawais, I was unaware of developments between the Explorer and a nearby ship. The other vessel was a plush yacht that had been chartered by a large surf clothing company for shooting the film featuring the pros we had encountered in the water. They were poorly anchored and the yacht kept on drifting closer to us, putting both vessels at risk. Our crew was beginning to get worried and eventually Gavin raised their captain on the radio. Unfortunately, the aggressive vibe that we had experienced in the water had also infected the crew of that yacht. The captain was not very friendly.

"Oi mate, who was 'ere first? I didn't come and drop anchor right next to you, did I? If you're not happy with my position, naff off then."

Gavin replied in much the same vein, banged down the receiver and shouted to those on deck, "Pull up the anchor! We're leaving."

"Hey Gav, André and Richard are still surfing," Francois called.

"Well, tell them to get the hell on out of the water. We're leaving."

After much gesticulating and shouting, the two surfers got the message, but of course it was difficult for them to just catch a wave immediately and come back. There was a lot of competition for every set and they continued to bob up and down in the line-up for a long time while waiting for an opportunity. They could have just paddled back to the ship, but they did not know why suddenly there was such urgency to leave and anyway, to paddle in instead of riding a wave to shore, or as in this case, closer to the ship, is another cardinal sin in surfing. Unless there's an emergency like an injury or a shark sighting, you don't paddle back. That is considered very bad form. Just as in life you finish a job off properly, in surfing you finish a session in style. That means riding a wave in. It's a matter of pride and principle. So André and Richard continued to wait for those final, elusive waves.

Gavin was not amused. "What are they waiting for, the blockheads? Call them again. This other joker will wreck us before long!"

But there was a lull at sea and all the surfers in the line-up sat idly, waiting for the next set.

"Right, that's it, I've had enough. Pull up the anchor, we're steaming away." Gavin was at the end of his tether.

"But they're not even close to us yet. Give them another five minutes," Francois remonstrated.

"Are you deaf? I said pull up the anchor! Or do you want to take over the captaincy? We'll steam over to the edge of the bay and wait for them there. They've had enough time to come back and they've chosen to laugh off my instructions. Now pull up the anchor."

And so we did. The Explorer moved away slowly just as the two surfers were making their way over to the ship. I looked at their perplexed faces as we moved into deeper water. They stopped paddling and sat up on their boards to see what was happening as we drew away from them. After a spell they started paddling again, amid derisive laughter from those aboard the other yacht.

Half an hour later Richard and André climbed on board, dehydrated and exhausted. Paddling across choppy water in the hot sun for that long on a short surfboard is no fun. Although they were never in danger during their paddle, the whole episode had been unnecessary and unpleasant. Now everyone had lost faith in Gavin's ability to continue as our captain.

"When does it become necessary to relieve a captain of his

duties?" Richard was quietly talking to Derek and Francois during their anchor watch that evening.

"We can do it if he's insane, otherwise it's mutiny. What the definition of insane would be, I don't know." He looked at Derek and me. Give us your medical opinion of him, Docs. Is he crazy enough to lock away?"

"I don't think so," Derek said. "I suppose the critical issue is whether he is endangering the ship and the rest of us or not. So far he's been impulsive and unpleasant, but not negligent or intentionally reckless. He hasn't caused any harm to us."

"He caused a lot of harm to my arms, pal. You paddle across that bay quickly and check it out. I won't be surfing tomorrow, that's for sure. And do you know how it feels to be abandoned on the ocean, not knowing where your ship is going? I'd like to jump on him while he's sleeping and tie him down just to make him worry a little in return. And what about that obsession he has with drinking water? Isn't there some psychiatric condition where people drink themselves to death just with water? Surely he's not normal."

"No, that's not enough to make him crazy. He's odd, but as far as I know, he is thinking rationally and the water thing is not affecting his decision-making when it comes to sailing the ship. We can't lock him away." Derek was adamant and I agreed with him.

"Shit, how nuts do you have to be before its official? Well, let's call a meeting and have it out with Gavin. I've had enough." With that Richard went to his cabin.

"I'll talk to Ron first." Francois was ever the diplomat. "He can prepare Gavin, so he doesn't just blow up at the meeting."

I followed Richard below to get some sleep while the other two continued talking in low voices.

Morning came and before a meeting could be called, Gavin announced that he was going ashore for some time to himself. Ron joined him and they set off along the water's edge.

"Now's our chance," Richard said. "Let's check out his cabin, that dark hole he never lets anybody into. That might give us some clues about what's going on in his head." Gavin's cabin was the only one with a proper wooden door and he kept it shut at all times. The rest of us had to make do with sarongs that we hung up in our doorways for privacy.

Derek and I followed Richard. The cabin looked gloomy, with a curtain drawn across the porthole, but from the doorway we could see rows of glistening objects lining the walls. Richard pulled aside the curtain and the sunlight revealed one of the weirder skippers' cabins you're likely to come across in the Indian Ocean. It was a shrine to water. Gavin had stacked water bottles everywhere he could fit them in. They were tied down with bungee cords in neat rows. Where the walls were visible between bottles, they had been covered with blue paper and the ceiling was pasted with posters of waves and seascapes. When you lay down on his bunk, all you saw was water and different shades of blue. It was obvious why Gavin had chosen to work at sea; he appeared to be infatuated with water.

We all stared at this for a while, but then my attention was drawn to a shelf with pill bottles. I looked closer and slowly it dawned on me why Gavin had become increasingly agitated and unwell the further we had sailed. There were two kinds of medication here, the malaria prophylactic mefloquine and some antidepressant tablets. Most of the mefloquine had been used, but there were still plenty of antidepressant tablets left.

"Look at this." I showed Derek the packets.

It took a few moments for the penny to drop and then Derek twigged. "Ahh, I see!"

"What?" Richard needed an explanation.

"These mefloquine tablets are what are driving Gavin crazy," I said. Sometimes they can lead to severe depression and even psychosis in susceptible people. And the other tablets are antidepressants. He's not taken many of them; look at how many he has left over. With a history of depression, he should never have been prescribed mefloquine."

"Do you think he's suffering from psychosis?"

"No, that's unlikely. He could just be very depressed. But

there are definitely some obsessive traits and hoarding behaviour here. All this water!"

"I don't understand all your mumbo-jumbo, Doc. Can we tie him up and cart him away or not?" He looked at me with a glint in his eye.

"No!"

"Aww, come on!" Richard looked like a child who had been told he couldn't go out to play. "Anyone who looks at this cabin will tell you there's a screw loose. He's off his rocker, missing a few marbles, one card short of a full house!"

"Personally, I quite like the way he has decorated his compartment, although it is somewhat cramped with all these bottles," Derek said. "If he stops the mefloquine and starts taking his antidepressant again, he could make a good recovery. He's not that bad."

"Oh, all right, if you want to take the nutter's side, but until he returns from Nih-nah land, he's not skippering this ship."

Derek and I had a conversation with Gavin and Ron acted as mediator.

"Yeah, I've always been prone to low moods, but I've been fine until recently. And then when I was starting to feel so low, I thought, 'Why take the stuff if it doesn't help?' So for the last month or so I didn't take any antidepressants."

"Your doctor should never have prescribed the mefloquine, knowing that you have depression," Derek said.

"Didn't tell 'em. I just got those in Singapore on the way down. Popped into a little clinic, told the nurse where I'm going and I didn't think depression counts as a serious illness, so I didn't mention it. Guess I messed up."

"At least the problem can be reversed once the mefloquine washes out of your system."

When we carefully broached the subject, Gavin seemed relieved to relinquish his responsibilities as captain for a while. "I could do with a bit of a break. Let Richard and Francois do the work for a while."

The tension on board that had been building over the

previous weeks eased, while Derek and I held thumbs that Gavin would recover without further intervention. It wouldn't be easy to find a psychiatric facility in these parts and if we did, the primary tools for treatment there would probably be handcuffs, a bucket of cold water and a pair of iron tongs.

We decided to stay put amongst the familiar islands for a while, so that things could settle down and over the next days we surfed a number of the well-known breaks: HT's, Lance's Left, Bank Vaults, Thunders and Rags. These waves were all very good, but they were often crowded. There were almost always other ships at anchor at the popular spots and the scenario was the same every time. The surfers had paid good money to be in the Mentawais and most of them were on a ten day charter. They were hungry for surf, with very little time to get their fill and they competed hard for waves. Most of the time everyone was friendly and the atmosphere in the water was pleasant, but it was a far cry from the empty perfection portrayed in the surf media or the deserted reefs we had found further north. I suppose every surfer starts surfing in order to experience the simple pleasure of sliding along a clean open face, but after a while I think one becomes relatively accustomed to the rush of the ride. Then we need something more: bigger waves, more challenging reefs, more remote spots and so on. There are also other, more peripheral aspects to surfing: just being in the water on a beautiful day, seeing the colour of the coral under the surface, watching birds glide by, meeting old friends in the water or simply being by yourself in a pleasant place. A surf session is an escape, a chance to forget our worries and frustrations and a reminder of how to enjoy life again. That is part of what made me leave the relatively crowded waters of the city in order to travel. But I found it difficult to feel the same exhilaration about life at spots where the crowd was often bigger than at many places I regularly surf around Cape Town. I missed the isolation of the more remote islands, even though we had not always had such a regular supply of waves there every day.

Still, one good wave at a break like HT's makes up for a lot and we spent quite a few days there, meeting the local villagers ashore and speaking to some surfers who were staying in the village of Katiet (land-crabbers they are now called). And of course we surfed that incredible wave. I thought about my first session, the hollow waves that were sucking off the reef and the beatings that I had endured there during my first weeks in the islands. Now I could surf these waves with a degree of confidence and every so often I managed a barrel. I was certainly not feeling over-confident in the water, but after three months in the islands I had come to a point where I managed to really enjoy the waves. This did make me a little complacent. As I took off on a good sized wave at HT's one day, I took a fraction of a second too long to get to my feet and that was enough for the wave to funnel away from me. The white water washed me in towards the reef and when I surfaced my heart sank as I saw a bigger wave rising up right in front of me.

Another surfer was just getting to his feet on this wave and we made eye contact for an instant – he the lucky one who was about to pull into the barrel and I, the poor wretch on the verge of receiving a proper rodgering as he sped towards Nirvana. After the wave had finished with me I ended up standing on the surgeon's table, somehow unhurt, but getting off it was the problem. I couldn't float above the reef, it was too shallow. I couldn't walk, because the reef was too uneven and waves surged over it at regular intervals, knocking my feet from under me. I stood in one place for a long time, bracing myself against each rush of white water that poured over the reef, waiting for a break between sets and seeing guys surfing just a few meters away from me. Finally, I managed to pick my way over the coral and into the channel.

Later, on board the ship, André asked, "Who was the sad sod standing there on the reef earlier on, didn't he know any better?"

"Ja, we had a good laugh at him doing the reef dance!" Johnno chuckled merrily.

"God knows," I said, "What an idiot."

Sometimes when we were surfed out, we'd sit on the back of the ship under the canvass, sip a warm Bintang and just watch the waves. There were some brilliant surfers in the water at times and it was an education just to see how a pro bends and contorts himself to become part of the wave, how he would disappear behind the curtain and reappear, making something so incredibly difficult look so effortless. But there were also the broken boards, the coral cuts and the bleeding limbs.

One afternoon while Derek was surfing, his board speared him in the face, cutting his lower lip open. The waves were perfectly clean and lined up. A good sized swell was running down the point and the rides were long and full of power. Derek sat up on his board and pulled his lip out as far as he could with his fingers, squinted down on it and declared that repairing it could wait. He sucked in his lip while he carried on surfing until the evening, when I had to stitch him up. The waves were just too good to cut the session short.

Gavin was spending less time below deck now and although he still kept to himself, his mood did seem to brighten gradually. He had given up carrying that little water bottle with him constantly and instead of wringing its neck when he felt uncomfortable, he now merely gripped his hands together. One evening after most people had gone to sleep, I caught him while he was returning some water bottles to the storeroom where they belonged. He just gave me a sheepish grin.

André, Sean and I had met another South African in the village. I forget his name now, but let's call him Jake. He had been travelling in South East Asia for a few months, taking busses and ferries to reach his destinations. Jake had long bleached hair, his body was decorated with mementos from different places he'd been to and from different girls he had come to know: pendants, bracelets, beads in his hair and a tattoo on his bum. (He refused to tell us how he got it.) Jake had a far-off look in his eyes when he spoke about places like Angkor Wat or the Perenthian Islands and he admitted that he had perhaps spent too much time in some of the towns with good herbs and interesting mushrooms. Jake's visit to Katiet was more out of necessity than due to an irrepressible desire to surf HT's. He liked to surf and he was heading to the Mentawais anyway, but he had ended up in this village after boarding a ferry out of desperation late one night. He had to escape a French girlfriend who wore only black and who was hooked on reading Sartre and anal sex. "She was smoking way too many joints and our relationship became a bit of a rough ride ... She was too intense, man."

Sean and I agreed with him that it was for the better that he had made his escape. Their love affair had become a bit of a bummer.

Because he was based on land, Jake could not just sail to another surf spot when the conditions changed, hence he knew of a path across the peninsula to the opposite side of the point. This spot was named Lance's Left, after the same guy who found HT's. Remember, HT's is also known as Lance's Right, after Lance Knight. (Yes, the sod found both spots. Nobody deserves to be that lucky!) When the wind is onshore at HT's, it would be offshore at the left on the other side. One morning when the wind turned bad and Richard was reluctant to leave the anchorage, the four of us put on our booties and board shorts, grabbed our surfboards and trudged out into the jungle. I wonder about the stories of sailors who spend so much time at sea on rolling ships that they can't walk properly on land. It never happened to any of us. The only person I ever knew who swayed back and forth on terra firma when he was sober was a weird guy from school who was excused from marching in military cadets because of a hip problem.

But we struggled to stay upright, nevertheless. It had been raining the night before and the path had been turned into a little river, with very slippery mud underfoot. I'd be walking along happily and suddenly my feet would simply slide out from underneath me, shooting up into the air like in a Charlie Chaplin movie. While I would still be rubbing my backside and wondering what had happened to me, one of the others would come slithering past me down the slope. Somewhere the path crossed a real river and we took the wrong option. We blundered forth into the burgeoning rain forest, thinking up several new swear words as we fell flat on our backs repeatedly. When you are carrying a surfboard, you always land harder than usual, because you protect the surfboard from damage at any cost. (You know that the graze on your buttocks will eventually heal up, but a damaged surfboard in a place like this might keep you out of the water for a long time and you just can't chance that.)

After an hour of making our way through the vines and spiky rattan plants without a parang to clear the way, we at last saw the sea glitter through the forest and we broke through onto the beach like Dr Livingstone and company. We half expected to find some cannibals cooking a missionary in a big black pot, but all that was visible was the sea, with clean looking three footers peeling along a reef in front of us, empty of surfers. We had found Lance's Left and we had it all to ourselves. Ahh, the anticipation ...

I managed to get to a green coconut that was hanging low down and we bashed it against a rock until it split open. We drank the sweet liquid and scooped out the white pulp with our fingers. This quenched our thirst and restored some of the energy we had expended on fighting the forest. Then we hit the shallows enthusiastically. The waves were fun, although the reef was quite shallow in the smallish conditions, so we were careful. It's often more dangerous to surf over a sharp reef when the waves are small. Bigger waves break in deeper water, giving you a little more leeway when you fall. After an hour in the water our bodies started to tingle and then to burn, especially our legs. First we thought the problem was sea lice, tiny organisms that make your skin itch all over, but then we saw the culprits all around us. Small, pink jelly-like creatures were pulsating in the water just behind the surf zone. Gradually, more and more of them arrived, and they seemed to be attracted to us. They headed straight for our dangling legs and they delivered a nasty sting whenever they got a chance. There were red welts everywhere they touched us and eventually they forced us to cut our session short. These nasty little customers were much smaller, but a lot more determined than the jellyfish we knew from back home. They were like little robots that had been sent to police the waves by some demented sea god. At least they weren't the lethal box jellyfish found in some parts of Indonesia and Australia. We knew this because we were all still alive, but it was no fun being harpooned by the tiny barbs on these jellies' tentacles and so we caught our last waves and headed for the beach, cursing them as we paddled.

The four of us sat on the pristine white sand and scraped out the last bits of coconut from its shell as we soaked up the sun. The glassy turquoise walls followed each other across the reef and collapsed into the shallows endlessly. Jake was studying the trees on the opposite shore of the little bay. "Hey, if a tree falls down in the forest and nobody hears it, does it really make a noise?"

"Oh, not that old cliché," Sean moaned, half asleep already. "Of course it makes a noise. The sound vibrates through the air whether someone is there to hear it or not."

"Well," said André, while brushing off the crusted salt from his shoulders, "I suppose the question is really whether something is meaningful if there is no one around to appreciate it. If the tree fell and nobody heard it, it may as well not have made a noise. There is no discernable difference from a human point of view."

Jake had been waiting for this opening. "Fully, Bru! Now, if you want to get all philosophical, you can ask the same thing about surfing. Sometimes the feelings and experiences you have while surfing are absolutely surreal, man. Like, you wonder if you didn't imagine it all. I mean, did you really just make it through that impossible section, or was it just a trick of the light that made the lip look like it was pitching in front of you? And did your fins really pop out on that radical turn, or was that sound a ligament in your knee that popped?"

He wasn't finished yet. "How 'bout if you get barreled off your nut on your own somewhere completely isolated? Did it really happen, or do you need an eyewitness to make it count?"

"Zzzzz, bo-oring." Sean wasn't impressed by our conversation.

"Perhaps the long hold down after your wipe-out made you hallucinate the whole ride," I mused. "And how many times haven't we all seen someone claim a spectacular tube ride when he was only squatting in the vicinity of the lip?"

Jake adjusted his position in the sand, digging in his hip a little deeper and stared at the trees for a while. "Ja, did any of it really happen? Let's be honest Bru, surfing never really produces any proof of our hard work, apart maybe from some bigger muscles. All that paddling … Ja, I scheme that's why the chicks dig me." He held up a scrawny arm and bulged his muscles. "An' here I thought it was my brilliant personality!" The rest of us had to chuckle.

He continued: "All that effort we put into searching for waves … We have nothing to show for our work, man. That is why photogs and filmmakers get so much respect. They are our witnesses, our only proof. Without them we can only blab on about our waves."

"And usually we bore our listeners to tears," Sean interjected. "But hey, if I got a good barrel, even if nobody else saw it, and you say it didn't happen, you'll know all about it!"

We opened another coconut, which we were enjoying when a charter yacht motored around the point and deposited five surfers in the water. They eagerly paddled into position and we watched them with equal eagerness for their reaction to the jellyfish. Soon enough our entertainment started and they slapped the water and were swearing with the kind of spirit that only the Aussies can muster. Rather than going back to their yacht, they surfed in over the reef and joined us under the palm trees. We exchanged stories about where we had been and compared jellyfish welts while having more coconut pulp. They were a group of friends from the north east of Oz who were all on the dole. Every one of them was careful not to find any permanent employment, because that would interfere with their surfing. The odd jobs they did on the side, together with their dole money, provided enough funds to pay for a surf charter every now and again. We glanced over at their yacht, which looked very sleek and comfortable and we could not blame these guys for not wanting to work. Why would you if your country provided a welfare system that enabled you to take dream holidays like this without lifting a finger?

When the swell gets small and the crowds become a little too much, the thing to do in the Mentawais is to head away from the usual spots visited by the charter boats on their regular milk run and to go south. We were told that The Hole was the spot that still sucked up swell when it became flat everywhere else and that it was just a little too out of the way for most ships to reach comfortably and still be within striking distance of the tried and trusted spots when the next swell arrived. Generally you'd have the place to yourself.

"Maybe Gavin would like the solitude there. It will be quiet and hopefully we won't have another yacht around," Michelle mused.

"As long as he doesn't wake me up in the middle of the night to catch rain water," was all Es said.

We set our course for the southern tip of Pagai Island. Although we knew more or less where the spot was, obviously nobody on board had ever been there and we weren't able to get co-ordinates or precise directions from other people we had spoken to. As with many other places we had found, there could potentially be a lot of searching involved and we needed a degree of luck as well. We did have a surf magazine with an article about the place, so we hoped that we could identify the necessary landmarks from the photos in the article. One thing that gave us a clue about the location was that there were some photos that had been taken from high up in the air and we were pretty sure that the writer of the article and his photographer colleague did not have access to a plane or helicopter. So we were looking for a tower or a mast of some kind. There were no high cliffs on these islands.

On our way to the Hole we anchored between two pretty little isles, uninhabited and with lots of potential for surf on a bigger swell, we thought. Francois and I launched the kayak and surveyed the area. Just beyond the point that protected our anchorage we saw a surfable wave running towards a tiny beach. This stretch of sand would disappear at high tide and we felt as if we had found a secret place. It would be hidden completely from passers-by when the next tide came in. What is more, the waves were breaking over sand, as opposed to coral, a pleasant novelty in the Mentawais. We quickly rowed back to the ship and grabbed our boards for a slow session in the tranquil surroundings. These waves would have been fun on a longboard, but we didn't have one with us. Still, it was good just to relax in the tepid water and to take in yet another perfect view. As the sun was setting, a large modern catamaran glided between the islands and dropped anchor nearby. Nick said hello to them on the radio. They were on their way back to Padang, spending their last night in the islands after a successful surf charter. They still had plenty of food left over and I suppose we looked hungry to them or maybe just a little rough around the edges, because the captain asked whether we would like some frozen lamb chops that they would not be eating. After so many weeks of sailing around the fringes of civilisation and only eating rice, vegetables and fish, lamb chops sounded completely exotic to us. The thought of sinking our teeth into firm red meat was utterly enticing. Although we really enjoyed the Eastern dishes we had been exposed to over the preceding months, there were certain things that our Western palates missed and we had already started experimenting with cheeseless pizza, coconut milk ice cream and a few other less successful dishes. Nick and André headed across to the cat in the tender before they could change their minds and they returned triumphantly with a big bag of booty. That night we all dreamt of the feast that was to come the following day. The main meal was scheduled for the evening and during the course of the day while we were busy with our daily tasks, we would stop doing what we were busy with, look at each other and say something like, "I wonder what's for supper this evening? Oh yes, lamb chops. Ha!" We could not wait.

The ship kept sailing south, heading for the Hole. This out of the way spot had a reputation as quite a hard breaking, intimidating wave. It's a lefthander that barrels from start to finish and it does not let you get away with any mistakes. If your take-off was too slow, or the line you set on the wave was not right, you'd get the usual Mentawai reef treatment, but with extra bite. A few of us natural footers started practicing our pig-dog stance on deck in anticipation.

It was mid afternoon when we arrived at a likely candidate for the Hole. A radio mast marked the spot and this was much more effective than any X on a pirate map. André and I stood at the base of the steel construction with our magazine open in front of us and we pinpointed the break. Unfortunately, the wind was onshore and the waves were small, making surfing there dangerous and unpleasant. Those of us who wanted to surf took the tender around a nearby headland where the wind would be more offshore, hoping for a consolation prize. After motoring up and down along the reef, four of us paddled out into the surf, but there was no safe place to leave the tender, so Richard headed back to the Explorer with instructions to pick us up two hours later. Our surf session was short lived. The swell was inconsistent and a fairly strong wind started to blow across the waves, making it virtually impossible to surf. We sat behind the breaking waves in a sullen ocean, looking down into murky water and feeling the chop slapping against our now goose-pimpled legs. Eventually we were all forced to paddle in to a small beach, where we waited for the tender to return. The tide had come up high onto the beach, squeezing us onto a corner of wet sand with mangrove trees on either side of us. There was nowhere to walk without wading through waist-deep water and the wind made it unpleasant to be out and about. Clouds moved in front of the sun and for the first time in the Mentawais we were feeling quite cold on our little patch of sand. I didn't know whether it was better to keep my wet rash vest on for warmth or to go bare-chested in the wind. We sat together and talked about various topics, like whether it had been worth coming all the way to the Hole, whether we would find waves there and what the conditions would be like over the next days, but time and again the conversation would return to one topic … lamb chops!

After what felt like ages, Richard came to pick us up in the tender. As we neared our ship, he slacked off on the throttle and we coasted closer the Explorer. "Do you boys smell what I smell? What could that be? Ah, roasted lamb!" All of us sat with our noses in the air like wolves scenting prey on the breeze. Mmm!

Derek had been entrusted with the task of preparing the important meal and he was waiting for us in the galley bare-arsed, wearing only an apron. Cooking lamb chops is clearly hot work. The table outside in the stern had been set with our red plastic plates, a hodgepodge of cutlery and some paper serviettes that had been dug out from somewhere. Melissa summoned everybody for dinner and showed us to our seats at designated places around the table. Then Derek appeared, still attired in his apron, but with a white pair of board shorts on his head now, like a chef's hat. He came around with a platter of hors d' oeuvres: "Ladies and gentlemen, we start with sardine a la Lucky Star, swimming in venerably aged tomato sauce. Only one each, I'm afraid." He set them down on our plates with a flourish. Derek had an (almost) white napkin over his arm and he walked around the table with a can of Bintang, asking each of us, "Would Sir like a glass of our finest with the meal?" He would then pour some beer into our plastic cups. After we had disposed of our starters (most of them were flung into the sea), it was time for some fruit salad. "Dear guests, to cleanse the palate, please have some tropical fruit delights," our Mâitre d' said. There were still some pieces of mango and paw-paw left in the fridge, with only a faint mouldy whiff to them. These were artistically decorated with bay leaves, the only available garnish. They left a fizzy, fermented kind of taste on the tongue.

Finally it was time for the main course. Derek and Melissa went around the table with two platters of lamb chops, carefully arranging them on our plates for maximum appeal. "Ladies and gentlemen, the moment you have all been waiting for has arrived," Derek announced. "Today we have delicately braised lamb chop, snugly nestled on a bed of Indonesian rice. Before we proceed however, I would like to ask the captain to say a few words." He bowed in Gavin's direction.

But all Gavin said was, "Chow down!" and we all attacked our chops like starved animals. The next few moments were passed in silence, with only a few grunts here and there. Everybody was very pleased with Derek's effort, but it was all over far too soon and as with most things, the anticipation had been the best part of the meal.

We sat around at the table in the dark (the spectacle of the setting sun had for once been upstaged by a few lamb chops) and we talked till late while picking the bones clean. Gavin stayed up with us, mostly just listening to everyone else's ramblings, but he smiled quietly to himself in a contented way. He seemed happier.

The following morning was bright and clear, with a slightly bigger swell running and no wind. I paddled over to the break from the ship with the sun on my back. The waves were clean, if a little on the small side, but it was good to be out with only a few of my fellow shipmates. I can't say that the session was exceptional, but our journey was nearing its end and we were trying to appreciate every wave we could get. It was good to at last feel comfortable in surf breaking over an unknown shallow reef. But the Hole had the final say and it claimed a prize. After an hour or so of surfing I came up after a close-out tube section had shut me down and found my board in two pieces. This was the end of this surfboard's life. Repairing it again was not an option. I couldn't really complain about it though. I had ridden so many waves on it in so many different places, sometimes subjecting it to very harsh treatment in big waves and it had survived. It had been given a new life in Lagundri after I had broken it the first time and it had continued to serve me well. Like so many other surfboards, it would never leave the Mentawais again (I eventually disposed of it in Padang) and that is not a bad place for a surfboard to end its days. Although, come to think of it now, maybe what to us is surfing heaven is hell to a surfboard, what with all the sharp reefs and heavy waves. Anyway, there were only a few more surfing days left for us and my two other surfboards would suffice.

It is hard to believe now, but towards the end of our journey I did start feeling ready to leave the Island Explorer. I wanted a change from the routines on board and I missed Anne a lot. At the time I made a point of remembering this feeling, because I knew that in the future I would want to be aboard that ship again and that I would romanticise the whole experience in my mind. We forget the hard parts and we focus on the good memories. That is fine, but remembering that our existence aboard was not perfect makes it easier for me now to carry on with life in the real world and not to wish for something that has passed.

Macaronis had still managed to elude us after all this time and we were willing to wait around in the area in order to catch it working. It was late afternoon when we arrived in the bay at that flawless lefthander just as another ship was leaving. There was nobody out. Some head high waves were winding down the reef in a light onshore wind. With about an hour and a half of daylight left, we knew that we'd have the waves to ourselves and as we were getting ready to jump into the water, we felt the wind dying.

Macaronis is known as a forgiving wave in the Mentawais, but I decided to strap on my helmet. Now was my chance to snag a backside barrel and I needed all the help I could get. The psychological lift of knowing that if I hit the reef my head would be protected would hopefully boost my confidence enough to get me into a tube.

I watched the swells as they started breaking at the top of the point, winding their way towards us steadily and mechanically, in an endless procession. Every wave was identical to the one before it, with no imperfections. It was as if the waves had been designed specifically for surfing, as if this place was an arena for the rituals required to appease Neptune. The bare, dead trees lining the point reached up towards the heavens with gnarled fingers, adding gravity to the atmosphere. None of us said anything. I think we were all in awe of the beauty before us.

As the sun dipped down towards the horizon, the water became completely glassy, the sky turned pink and the waves became flawless. They were so smooth that there was hardly any sensation as you skimmed along the surface on your surfboard. You could hold your fingers just above the wall you were riding and feel the pulse of the wave.

I stroked into a few rollers and wound my way down the reef with them, getting a good feeling for the energy and pace of the waves. On my way back to the take-off area I paddled slowly, preparing myself for what I had been waiting for all this time: attempting to pull into a backside barrel well behind the curtain and coming out again. A half-second cover-up behind an errant section of lip would not do. It had to be an undisputed tube ride.

I sat away from the others in the water, looking at the horizon while the swells that moved beneath me lifted me up and down slowly. On my next wave I was going to go for the tube, I said to myself. I let a number of good waves pass before turning around and pushing down the face of a four-footer that swung a little wider than the rest. My feet found the perfect position on my board and I turned off the bottom smoothly, came back up into the pocket and I set my line for the tube. A little pressure on my back foot and suddenly I was inside a black tunnel, headed for the pink sky. As I came nearer to the shoulder of the wave, I stalled a little more and once again the falling lip cascaded ahead of me. The wave echoed and sighed inside my helmet, and for a brief moment I held on to the bliss of being inside that hallowed place, then my board glided out, taking me along.

I emerged from the tube to hoots and cheers from Sean, Johnno, Derek and Richard, who all sat right in front of me in the channel. It felt like I had finally been initiated into their clan. They had witnessed this tube ride first hand. Now I could really say that I could surf!

Nobody ever rode a smoother, slicker wave than that one and though the ride was over mere seconds after I got to my feet, the memory of the experience has lasted, becoming better every year. By now literally thousands of surfers would have done what I had done at Macaronis; this was by no means a unique achievement. But it was my first proper backside barrel over shallow coral at a world-class spot and the feeling was indescribable. I had gone to heaven.

That evening we celebrated my tube ride again and again. Everybody was happy for me.

Our last surf was at HT's for old time's sake. The obligatory posse of pro's was also skulking around the line-up, most of them happy to be there, but some of them glum and morose. It reminded me that in the end it did not matter so much where you are in the world or how good your surroundings are. What is important is how you feel, what is going on in your mind. Happiness can be found anywhere if your attitude is right. As long as you accept your situation and make peace with the world around you, you can achieve a state of bliss in the worst slums and in the ugliest places. Sure, it helps if you happen to be in a barrel at the time. But I saw too many brilliant surfers who were getting waves that were way better than anybody else's, but who stayed unfulfilled. They were in paradise, but they did not allow themselves to enjoy the experience. You may be in Nirvana, but you won't see it if you don't have the right frame of mind. Marcel Proust said, "The real voyage of discovery consists not in seeking new landscapes but in having new eyes."

Ultimately, I think the driving force behind everything we want to do is a yearning for happiness. No matter what the goal, we hope that if we manage to attain it, that it will make us happy.

But whichever method you use to attain fulfilment, be it philosophy, religion or chasing waves, does not matter. In the end, you have to accept your situation and be happy with who you are and where you are. For me that is the biggest challenge.

I loved the Mentawai islands and I still dream about that magical archipelago in the Indian Ocean. If I were single and fancy-free, I would probably have ended up living somewhere along the shore of a quiet little island, out of the way of the world. But luckily I have found something better in the people that surround me. I am happier at home with them, even though home isn't all tropical beaches, balmy evenings and glassy waves. As an often repeated aphorism goes, I had travelled all over the globe, only to discover that the thrills and the joy that I was looking for were not in a far-off, exotic land, but locked up inside myself.

The final evening on the Island Explorer arrived and Nick asked Gavin to pilot the ship back to port for the last time. "You are the captain after all, hey Gav?"

"Sure," said Gavin, and he gave Nick his old skew smile. He set the course for Padang and shouted, "Pull up the anchor!" For the last time we all lined up on deck, took hold of the rope and heaved.

We motored into the evening in the opposite direction that we had taken more than three months before on that stormy, dark night. This time, however, the sea was calm and smooth. The only coolness was provided by the light breeze that was created by the ship's movement into the darkness.

I don't remember who decided to clean out all the cupboards in the galley, but some half-empty bottles of Arak, local brandy and palm wine were found and brought out onto the deck. We had run out of beer a few days previously, so the excuse of emptying out the bottles that were supposedly cluttering the ship seemed like quite a good idea. Although all of us were looking forward to meeting friends ashore, travelling on to different destinations or just to get home, I think we all felt like drowning our sorrows just a little. We were very lucky that on the whole all of us got on well. We had our highs and our lows, but for a bunch of strangers thrown together almost at random, we had done pretty well. Everybody felt sad to see the others go. In my case, there were strongly mixed feelings. At last I would see Anne again. She was flying to Malaysia, where we would meet up and then travel a little more. I had been planning our itinerary for a few weeks already and now that it was almost time to meet, I really couldn't wait to see her. Even the most perfect waves in the world eventually lose their appeal if you don't have a soul-mate to share your experiences with.

And there were some minor irritants that I would be happy to be rid of. Anchor pulling in the dead of night, the empty hours of staring at windblown seas with nothing to do and the chores of keeping a ship running had become tiresome to me. I was ready to move on.

But the fantastic dream that I had been living for the past few months was now ending and I knew that it would be almost impossible to repeat such an experience again in my lifetime. It was unlikely that I would see my shipmates again. This was the end of an incredible period of freedom, discovery and of learning for me. I was about to return to real life, back from Wonderland, and I was closing a door behind me that I would not be able to open again. There were countless things that I had learned about surfing on this trip, but I had learned so much more than that. I had graduated from Ron's University of the Real World.

The bottles of Arak were passed around on the foredeck and we sampled the sticky, syrupy liquids. After a few sips, we got used to the sickly sweet taste. We even started liking it and before we knew, everyone was quite jolly, drinking various concoctions in ever increasing quantities. For the last time, we threw caution to the wind as the ship floated onwards.

Our party was interrupted only momentarily by Gavin who told us to stop rugby tackling each other on deck, as we were getting dangerously close to the sides of the ship and that the last thing he wanted now was someone falling overboard. Cutting that game short was a good thing, because a number of us discovered some nasty bruises and grazes on various parts of our bodies the following morning. We slowed down for a while, lying under the stars that initially had been so strange to us. By now we had come to know these constellations from many anchor watches and from the hot, humid evenings spent on deck. We were stretched out on our backs and we studied them for the last time, becoming a little melancholy with the thought that soon they would only be a vague memory. But evenings never stay dull for long when Francois and André are around and Arak is a very activating drink. The night wore on until Melissa came up from her and Derek's cabin, furious after I had accidentally dropped a plate full of noodles through their hatch and caught her full in the face while she was sleeping. We went to bed after that, hell hath no fury …

As I lay rocking in my bunk for the last night on the Selat Mentawai, smelling the briny air and listening to the creaking of the Explorer's rigging and its ironwood planks, I thought of this voyage that had lured me in and taken me along on an adventure that I would never have been able to dream up. I took stock of my accomplishments. What of my hopes to go to a completely isolated, primal place and to have a truly wild experience? No, that didn't happen. Some of the places we had visited were pretty untamed, but they weren't exactly Jurassic Park either. Would I have been happier in the long run if we did make landfall on some secluded island where the natives wore animal skins and hunted with bows and arrows? No, probably not, although it would have been a great story to tell. And who knows, one day I might still get the chance. Part of me will always keep on travelling amongst this archipelago.

When I woke up the following morning, the Island Explorer was moored in the same spot in the bay outside Padang as when I first saw it. The water around us was calm and as smooth as a mirror, the air thick, pungent and hot – hotter than in the outer islands. I looked out of my porthole and watched some workers as they loaded goods onto nearby ships. The hill in the background was green with Mimosa bushes and I imagined them contracting their leaves as birds brushed past them, causing a cascade of movement up the slope, like Leipoldt had imagined it all those years ago. A heavily-laden truck slowly struggled up the road that leads to the city, belching smoke and moving more or less at the speed of an ox-cart. Here in the bay things had not changed all that much since the early nineteen-hundreds. I swung my legs off my bunk to get up and, as had been the case so many times before, I felt nauseous. But now, for the first and the last time during my adventure on board the Island Explorer, my nausea was not caused by seasickness.

The End

About the Author

Dan Scheffler lives just outside Cape Town, South Africa with his wife and son.

He is a doctor in general family practice, but tries not to let work interfere too much with his surfing.

When the Cape winters get cold or the Southeaster howls incessantly in summer, he escapes by writing about wild places and tropical trips.

Connect with Dan Scheffler:

trippybooks@gmail.com
islandexplorerbook.com
danscheffler.wordpress.com/
facebook.com/pages/Dan-Scheffler/521593047867330
smashwords.com/profile/view/danscheffler
amazon.com/Dan-Scheffler/e/B00979ESEO

Made in the USA
Charleston, SC
17 December 2012